The Great Automation

The Great Automation

Surviving the Age of Intelligent Systems

Kenan Durveil

Mindful Pages

Published in 2026

ISBN: 9789374592861 (PB)
ISBN: 9789374599143 (eBook)

Published by

Mindful Pages
Imprint of Alpha Editions LLC
312 W. 2nd St #1834
Casper, WY 82601, USA

This book was developed using advanced writing tools to support the drafting and ideation process. All content has been thoughtfully curated, refined, and reviewed to ensure quality and relevance.

Content

Introduction

The shift was almost imperceptible at first: a quiet warehouse on the outskirts of a provincial town, the sort of place usually noted only when delivery vans queue at the gates. Inside, five workers moved deliberately between shelves while a fleet of small, wheeled robots darted in smooth arcs across the polished floor. Together, this tiny team picked, sorted, and dispatched more orders in a single afternoon than a hundred people once managed on their busiest day. The lights remained dim, humming low to save power; the robots did not mind. The workers, though, were alert, wary, carrying the strange tension of people whose roles had narrowed even as the enterprise expanded. Productivity soared. Morale frayed. For many, it felt like standing in the shadow of progress, close enough to see the benefits but never quite touched by them.

You can find variations of this scene across factories, hospitals, back offices, design studios, call centres, and classrooms. Automation has begun to move not only boxes and parts but also words, data, images, decisions. Machines grow sharper in perception and quicker in response, while many human roles have been squeezed into ever tighter corners. A paradox has settled over modern work: as systems grow smarter, many jobs feel smaller. The tools are brilliant; the people often feel diminished. Anxiety rises quietly, like background radiation. Burnout accelerates. Wages stagnate even as output climbs. The distance between what technology promises and what workers experience widens by the year.

This book begins within that tension. Not to lament it, nor to offer consoling myths, but to chart a different path altogether. The central argument is simple: humans are not disappearing. Human value is changing shape. The decline is not in our worth, but in the architectures of work that have failed to adapt to a new kind of partner—intelligent systems capable of sensing, analysing, and acting with startling speed. When the environment changes but the structure of opportunity does not, individuals feel squeezed. The point, therefore, is not to resist automation but to redesign how we participate in it.

The story of automation is often told as a clash between labour and machines, as though history were a series of battles in which tools wrest roles from flesh and blood. Yet, for centuries, technology has also liberated people from drudgery and opened paths to greater imagination. Gutenberg's press did not erase scribes; it multiplied readers. The industrial loom did not extinguish textile knowledge; it reshaped craft into design, distribution, and enterprise. The paradox of progress—its gifts and its disruptions—has always been with us. What makes this moment distinctive is that automation has crossed an invisible threshold. It no longer stops at muscle. It competes, sometimes elegantly, with cognition.

A machine can now review thousands of legal documents, generate a marketing campaign in minutes, draft code, translate languages, diagnose certain conditions, summarise meetings, and suggest interventions in complex systems. It does not sleep or take offence. It learns patterns at scale and whispers recommendations into dashboards, inboxes, and interfaces. At first glance, this seems to threaten the very foundation of human contribution. But look again and a different picture emerges. Automation excels in replication and prediction. It stumbles in ambiguity, ethics, story, taste, and the fragile art of human relationship. The highest value now lies not in what a machine can do, but in what a machine cannot decide.

What follows in the pages ahead is not a manifesto of optimism or despair, but a guide to agency. The questions that animate this book are practical and urgent. How does one build a career in a world where knowledge is cheap but judgement is rare? What does it mean to work with systems that increasingly shape outcomes before we even notice their suggestions? How should organisations adapt when small teams with powerful tools can outperform large ones burdened by legacy structures? And how might societies ensure that the benefits of automation flow not merely to platforms and shareholders but to workers, communities, and citizens?

These questions touch everyone, regardless of sector or seniority. A junior analyst using automated dashboards must decide when to trust a model and when to challenge it. A nurse using clinical decision support tools must navigate the intersection of evidence, experience, and empathy. A designer exploring concepts with generative models must choose not just what looks good, but what tells a coherent story. A manager overwhelmed by digital noise must learn to orchestrate teams and tools rather than react to every alert. The thread running through all these tasks is the same: human value now resides in the spaces above automation, not beneath it.

To understand how to thrive in this landscape, we must first recognise the nature of the shift. Automation is no longer a bolt-on efficiency; it has become an architectural layer. Many of the world's most influential systems—financial markets, supply chains, media platforms, healthcare providers—operate as hybrids of human judgement and algorithmic coordination. Decisions that once moved slowly through hierarchical chains now crackle across networks of sensors, models, and workflows. What we are witnessing is the rise of what might be called *machine judgement*: systems that do not simply calculate but interpret signals and recommend actions that shape real-world behaviour. For individuals, this introduces both leverage and vulnerability. Leverage, because access to such systems can multiply one's output dramatically. Vulnerability, because a poorly understood model can propagate errors far beyond one's intention.

A recurring motif in this book is a simple yet powerful distinction: the difference between automation that compresses human roles and automation that expands them. Compression happens when systems take over tasks without redesigning the work around them; workers are left managing exceptions, troubleshooting failures, and absorbing stress. Expansion happens when automation is paired with clear human decisions, creative freedom, and well-designed workflows. In those environments, people move from repetitive execution to higher-order thinking: framing problems, curating outputs, shaping narratives, negotiating context, and exercising ethical judgement. The promise of automation lies not in replacing labour but in elevating it—if we choose to build systems that make this possible.

Historical echoes matter here. Every major technological transformation—mechanisation, electrification, digitalisation—has forced societies to renegotiate the relationship between skill, value, and identity. But none has done so as quickly as this one. The current wave of intelligent systems evolves at a pace that leaves little time for the slow, generational adaptation that cushioned earlier disruptions. We cannot wait for institutions to catch up; the responsibility for adaptation now falls directly on individuals, teams, and organisations. This is not a counsel of abandonment but a call for deliberate design. The future is not something that happens to us; it is something we shape through the choices we make in how we work, learn, and share power.

At the centre of this book is a belief that skills can compound. Judgement improves with practice. Taste sharpens through exposure and critique. Relationships strengthen through consistency. Learning accelerates when it is woven into daily routines rather than treated as occasional training. These are not soft assets; they are the bedrock of resilience in a world of shifting tools and volatile markets. The irony of the automation age is that the most human skills—those tied to perception, meaning, and moral choice—are becoming the most economically valuable. Machines generate options. Humans decide what matters.

This introduction also gestures toward a broader societal question: what do we owe each other in an age of intelligent systems? If automation amplifies inequality, concentrates power in a handful of platforms, and fragments communities, then technical progress alone will not deliver collective prosperity. We must examine the social contract that governs work, reward, and opportunity. Policies that protect workers and encourage innovation need not be opposites; indeed, they are mutually reinforcing. When individuals feel secure enough to take risks, economies become more dynamic. When organisations invest in people, not just tools, performance improves. When citizens have visibility into how algorithms influence public life, trust grows. The stakes extend far beyond individual careers to the health of democratic societies.

A metaphor lingers throughout this book: the idea of an *operating system for work*. Every worker, team, and institution runs on one—some explicit, others tacit. It is the combination of routines, principles, tools, and habits that govern how decisions are made. In the automation age, many existing operating systems are misaligned with the capabilities of new tools. They were built for slower cycles, narrower information flows, and clearer boundaries between human and machine. The task before us is to write a new one—not through technical wizardry alone, but through careful attention to ethics, culture, learning, and design.

As we stand at this juncture, the future feels both exhilarating and unsettling. Intelligent systems are accelerating the pace of change, challenging the assumptions underpinning our education systems, our organisations, and even our personal identities. Yet this uncertainty also contains latent opportunity. The next decade could be an age of remarkable human flourishing—if we make the right choices. The chapters ahead offer practical frameworks, detailed cases, and strategic tools to help you shape those choices. They are not abstract theories but grounded, actionable approaches tested across contexts: from small businesses using automation to compete with much larger rivals, to professionals redesigning workflows to reclaim time and focus, to communities and institutions crafting new norms for fairness, transparency, and dignity.

What will your role be in this landscape? Will automation narrow your work, or widen it? Will you allow systems to dictate your value, or will you define the parts of your craft that matter most? When intelligent assistants produce competent first drafts in seconds, what will differentiate you? When algorithms steer decisions in your workplace, how will you maintain agency? When new tools emerge faster than institutions can regulate them, who will ensure that their use aligns with human wellbeing rather than convenience alone?

These are not distant hypotheticals. They are the pressures shaping daily life. And they are the reason this book exists—not to offer reassurance, but to offer capability. The future of work belongs not to those who outrun machines, but to those who learn to guide them. To those who understand that automation is a multiplier of intention. To those who can wield judgement, taste, empathy, and learning as durable advantages. To those who recognise that the purpose of technology is not to compress human lives into narrower roles, but to expand the realm of what we can imagine and achieve.

As you move into the main chapters, hold one question close: *What becomes possible when automation is not your rival, but your amplifier?* The answer, as you will discover, is both practical and profound. The systems we build shape who we become. And the future, still unwritten, remains within our reach.

Chapter 1
The Shape of the Shift

The robot did not look like much: a neat, knee-high cube gliding between shelving units, pausing only to swivel its sensors or to let a human pass. Yet every movement it made—every turn, every retrieval, every decision about the most efficient route—expressed a subtle transfer of agency. Once, warehouse pickers decided how to navigate the aisles, which order to prioritise, when to pause, and when to accelerate. Now the cobot handled these micro-judgements quietly, continuously, and with increasing sophistication. The humans nearby were no longer orchestrators of motion but supervisors of exceptions, stepping in only when the machine encountered something it could not interpret. The rhythm of work had changed; so had its meaning.

Some kilometres away, in a modest marketing team wedged between a café and a co-working space, another kind of machine rendered its own verdicts. Feed it campaign goals, customer segments, and a library of historic data, and it would produce variations—hundreds, then thousands—testing headlines, images, tone, pacing, and audience triggers. The team had once brainstormed these elements from scratch. Now they sifted through outputs, weighing which carried the right note of wit or restraint. The machine had become a collaborator of sorts, generating possibilities at a volume no human could match. Yet the responsibility still rested with the marketers to choose what was appropriate, strategic, or ethical. Their craft shifted from creation to curation.

These two scenes—one industrial, one creative—suggest a deeper pattern shaping modern work. Automation has migrated from tools that simply *execute* to systems that *choose*. From mechanisation to judgement. From straightforward levers and scripts to software that senses the environment, interprets it, and acts on the interpretation. This transition is subtle enough to escape the eye yet profound enough to unsettle professional identity across every sector. When machines begin to decide, even in small, localised ways, human roles evolve. Sometimes they shrink. Sometimes they expand. Much depends on how the shift is understood and designed.

We are living through the emergence of what might be called *machine teammates*—not out of sentimentality, but out of structural accuracy. These systems are not conscious; they have no intent. But their influence on work now resembles the influence of colleagues: they offer suggestions, shape priorities, establish rhythms, and constrain or expand what feels possible. The heart of this chapter lies in exploring exactly that shift: how tools became something closer to teammates, how judgement migrated from people to processes, and why this matters not only for productivity but for power, agency, and meaning.

To grasp the significance of this moment, we need to pull back and view the landscape from its origins.

Mechanisation once replaced muscle. Machines lifted, pressed, cut, and carried. They robbed no one of cognitive autonomy and seldom altered the nature of decision-making. An assembly-line worker did not wonder whether the conveyor belt held implicit views about optimal sequencing. The tool was obedient, almost inert. The human mind remained sovereign.

The digital revolution complicated matters. Software captured rules and followed them at speed. Still, the logic came from human designers. The spreadsheet did not infer; it calculated. The script did not adapt; it executed. For decades, automation was a matter of efficiency rather than epistemology: a faster way to apply known rules to known problems.

What changed was prediction. As models began to learn from data rather than instructions, automation slipped into domains once assumed to require human judgement. Instead of programming a system to classify an image, we fed it millions of examples and allowed it to infer patterns. Instead of telling a model how to draft a paragraph, we trained it on linguistic histories and let it anticipate the next plausible word. What emerged were tools capable not only of processing information but of *interpreting* it—an ability that blurred the line between execution and choice.

This shift carries immense consequences for everyday work. In practical terms, people now operate within environments where decisions are distributed: partly human, partly machine, and partly the interactions between them. The decisions may be small—predicting the likelihood of a customer churning, proposing a design layout, recommending an appointment slot—but together they reshape the contours of labour. When routines become automated, what remains for people are the higher-order tasks: defining goals, resolving ambiguity, negotiating tensions, and applying taste. Many find this liberating. Others find it disorienting. Some organisations redesign roles to support this new reality; others attempt to force old structures onto new systems and watch their staff drown in exception management and incoherent workflows.

Economists, for their part, have long mapped output as a function of capital and labour. The neatness of that model has now fractured. A third factor—algorithms—has entered the scene. Not as a subset of capital, nor as a replacement for labour, but as a distinct source of leverage. Cheap prediction alters cost curves in ways that feel almost alchemical. Consider the small firm suddenly able to match a far larger rival by integrating off-the-shelf AI tools into its processes. The gap in headcount matters far less when software can handle segmentation, generate proposals, analyse financials, and surface insights with minimal prompting. The competitive frontier shifts from scale to architecture: the ability to assemble a nimble configuration of people and systems.

This is not merely a business story; it is a power story. Every shift in the production function redistributes advantage—sometimes subtly, sometimes violently. Automation's benefits leak through multiple channels: prices may fall, profits may rise, time may be freed. But these gains do not flow evenly. They pool in certain places and evaporate in others. For the rideshare driver whose income depends on a dispatch algorithm, the asymmetry is stark. The algorithm allocates jobs, sets incentives, shapes routes, and ultimately governs earnings. The driver contributes labour, but the levers of value sit elsewhere. Unless rules and design choices counteract concentration, technological leverage tends to centralise rather than disperse power.

The chapter you are about to explore follows these threads with care. It traces the migration from tools to teammates, showing how machine judgement now shapes the texture of work. It examines the new production function and explains why algorithms deserve recognition as a third factor of output. It maps winners, losers, and the delicate leaks through which value escapes or accumulates. And it returns, repeatedly, to a foundational question: what remains distinctly human in this evolving landscape?

Human advantage still exists. Indeed, it is growing more precious as automation expands. Certain capabilities—framing problems, exercising ethical discernment, applying taste, nurturing relationships—resist replication not because machines lack raw processing power, but because these qualities arise from context, meaning, and lived experience. They are relational rather than computational. Consider the chef experimenting with recipe-generation tools. The model can propose combinations and techniques, drawing on culinary history and pattern recognition. But the act of curating a menu—balancing the room's atmosphere, the story of the ingredients, the expectations of diners, and the emotional arc of the meal—draws on sensibilities far beyond algorithmic reach. Judgement sits above generation.

This distinction becomes a quiet motif throughout the chapter: machines can multiply options, but only humans can decide which *ought* to prevail. In a world saturated with outputs, the value of discernment rises.

As this introduction closes, you stand at the threshold of a complex yet empowering shift. The next pages will show how automation restructures not just tasks but the very logic of work. They will reveal how decisions migrate, how value concentrates, and how human capabilities can either wither or flourish depending on the systems built around them. You will see how the warehouse cobot, the marketing AI, the small firm leveraging prediction, the rideshare driver negotiating algorithmic oversight, and the chef curating a menu all form part of a single, sweeping transformation.

What is changing is not simply the nature of tools, but the nature of agency. And as you move deeper into the chapter, one question should linger in your mind, sharp and unresolved: when machines can sense, decide, and act, what becomes the true shape of human work?

From tools to teammates

In March 2021, Ocado Group opened a redesigned fulfilment centre in Erith, south-east London. The organisation reported that more than a thousand squat, battery-powered robots zipped across its grid of crates, each unit calculating routes, adjusting speed, and selecting items with barely a pause. The human workers on site noticed the shift most clearly not in the volume of orders—though these rose sharply—but in the way decisions moved. The system determined which crates surfaced, where staff should stand, and when to intervene. People no longer guided the flow; they responded to it. One engineer described it as "working inside a machine that thinks", a phrase that captured a broader transformation spreading well beyond logistics. Something fundamental had changed: the tools were beginning to decide.

The scene at Erith was neither novelty nor spectacle. It marked a threshold in the quiet evolution of automation from mechanisation to something closer to judgement. To grasp the scale of this shift, consider the question that hovered over the warehouse floor: how does a system without consciousness still shape the behaviour of those around it? The answer lies in the pattern of micro-choices the robots executed—route selection, collision avoidance, dynamic task assignment. These judgements once belonged exclusively to people. Now they emerged from models, sensors, and optimisers reacting in real time. The shift was subtle. It was also seismic. And it suggested a motif that threads through this section: the machine as *partner* in decision-making rather than a mere extension of muscle.

For much of industrial history, machines imitated force, not thought. The steam engine at Soho Manufactory in Birmingham in 1788 replaced arduous labour but not human discretion. The loom did not interpret fabric patterns; the worker did. Even the early waves of digital automation preserved this hierarchy. Scripts written in the 1980s and 1990s performed predefined tasks—calculations, transfers, formatting—but only under explicit instructions. They did not adapt or infer. Their value came from predictability, not autonomy. Human judgement remained chief steward of complexity.

What has unfolded since roughly 2015 is a decisive turn. Advances in sensor arrays, reinforcement learning, and large-scale predictive models shifted the boundary of what machines could *perceive*. Instead of following fixed rules, systems now learn from data captured in the wild: images, purchase histories, user interactions, warehouse movements. A warehouse cobot that slows when a human approaches behaves not because a programmer stipulated every scenario, but because its model inferred risk from thousands of examples. In a narrow but real sense, the machine has formed expectations about its environment. Whether those expectations are correct is another matter entirely, and one that shapes the reliability and ethics of automation.

The marketing world offers an instructive parallel. In early 2022, the cosmetics company Lush trialled an AI-assisted creative workflow at its Poole headquarters. The model analysed historic campaigns, customer engagement patterns, and seasonal trends. It suggested concepts at a scale the human team could not match. More strikingly, it prioritised its proposals based on inferred audience reactions. The creative staff remained responsible for the final selection, but crucially, the range of *initial* options—the cognitive raw material—was determined by the system. A form of judgement had migrated from people to processes: what should be considered at all.

This migration matters deeply to everyday work. When systems regularly pre-sort information, recommend actions, or decide sequencing, they alter the terrain on which human expertise operates. The shift is not total; nor is it uniform. But it is pervasive, shaping roles from retail to law, from design to customer service. It invites a rethinking of agency. If a system anticipates a customer's next move before a representative speaks to them, who is really setting the tone of the interaction? If a model flags high-risk legal clauses in a contract, how does the lawyer's attention redistribute? When a cobot chooses its own route, what becomes of the worker's tacit knowledge of the floor layout? Agency has not disappeared. But it has been redistributed.

None of this is accidental. It arises from a deeper engineering shift: automation has become probabilistic rather than deterministic. Older systems followed instructions. Newer systems forecast. The distinction matters because forecasts are judgements about uncertainty. A predictive model in a supply chain forecasts demand for a Saturday in Leeds. A content-ranking algorithm infers that a viewer in Edinburgh is more likely to watch a documentary than a thriller on a given evening. These predictions guide allocation of staff, goods, and attention. They may be right; they may be wrong. But the decisions they trigger can ripple widely.

A counter-example, however, offers caution. In 2019, the Netherlands Tax and Customs Administration deployed an automated fraud-detection system intended to identify high-risk childcare benefit claims. A parliamentary inquiry later found that the model disproportionately flagged families with dual nationality, generating wrongful accusations and causing severe financial harm. The system did not "decide" in any moral sense. Yet its outputs carried weight. Its probabilistic logic was mistaken, and its consequences fell on people with little recourse. The case illustrates a limit: when machine judgement is accepted too readily, errors can scale further and faster than in purely human systems.

Reconciling this limitation with the promise of automation requires clear boundaries. The role of the system must be visible. The locus of accountability must remain human. Where these principles hold, machines can deepen capability without diluting responsibility. Where they fail, systems become brittle, opaque, and prone to replicating bias at speed.

The economic implications of this shift are equally pronounced. A system that decides changes cost dynamics. It compresses the time between sensing and acting. It reduces the labour required for coordination. And it introduces a new category of capital: *algorithmic capital*, whose performance improves with experience rather than wear. This reframes competition. A small firm in Manchester using off-the-shelf predictive models for forecasting or customer segmentation can, by mid-2023 standards, match decisions once reliant on departments of analysts. The boundaries of scale blur. What once required dozens of people now requires a handful with a well-crafted workflow. As decision-making becomes modular and codified, organisational advantage hinges on assembling the right constellation of people and systems rather than amassing headcount.

Yet even here, a quiet tension persists. Decisions made by systems are often accepted uncritically because they appear neutral. But neutrality is an illusion. Every model encodes assumptions: which data matters, which outcomes count, which patterns deserve weight. In the Ocado warehouse, the cobots optimise for speed and density. They do not weigh the cognitive load of humans navigating around them. In Lush's creative trials, the model prioritised engagement metrics; it could not measure whether a concept aligned with the organisation's values around ethical sourcing or social impact. These omissions are not technical defects. They are reminders that machine judgement is incomplete by design.

This leads back to the motif of the *teammate*. A good teammate contributes strength without overriding judgement. A poor teammate creates friction or distorts collective purpose. The same is true for automated systems. Their impact depends on how humans integrate them: whether as collaborators that extend ability or as replacements that narrow it. The difference lies not in technology alone but in workflows, incentives, and culture.

Consider a rideshare driver operating in Bristol in 2022. The dispatch algorithm, housed thousands of miles away, determines which passenger they collect next, how much they will earn for the journey, and whether their acceptance rate affects future opportunities. The driver supplies labour and local knowledge. The system supplies coordination and demand prediction. But the balance of power is uneven. The algorithmic teammate is inscrutable, uncommunicative, and immune to negotiation. Its priorities—minimising wait times, balancing supply, maximising platform revenue—may not align with the driver's need for predictable income or safe working patterns. The example underscores a central question for this section: what happens when the teammate cannot be reasoned with?

Contrast this with a marketing analyst at a midsize firm in Leeds using a generative model to test variations of a product pitch. The system proposes options, but the analyst chooses which idea to refine based on brand knowledge, cultural fluency, and ethical considerations. Here, the teammate extends capacity but does not subsume agency. The dynamic is collaborative rather than extractive.

The tension between these two arrangements—augmentative versus controlling—defines much of the debate about automation's role in work. Tools that sense, decide, and act can elevate human capability when the boundaries are clear and the distribution of agency is fair. They can also hollow out roles when they impose decisions rather than inform them. The heart of the matter lies in design choices: transparency, override mechanisms, clear audit trails, and the deliberate recognition that not all decisions should migrate to processes.

The story of mechanisation was straightforward: machines replaced muscle. The story of machine judgement is more subtle. It is the story of tools that shape context before work begins. It is the story of systems that generate alternatives before humans think to ask for them. It is the story of decisions that occur upstream, shifting the terrain on which expertise operates. And it is the story of a world where agency becomes shared—sometimes wisely, sometimes not.

The motif of the teammate returns here. A teammate extends what you can do, but only if you understand what they can and cannot handle. The same applies to automated systems. They excel at pattern recognition; they falter in ambiguity, ethics, and story. They handle volume; they struggle with meaning. They propose; they do not care. The challenge—and opportunity—is to shape workflows where the strengths of systems and the strengths of people align rather than collide.

As this section moves forward, one question hovers unresolved, like the faint hum of a cobot gliding across the warehouse floor: when responsibility, power, and judgement distribute between humans and systems, how do we decide which decisions must remain ours?

The new production function

When Ronald Coase published *The Nature of the Firm* in November 1937 at the London School of Economics, he did not imagine algorithms as factors of production. His question was disarmingly simple: why do firms exist at all when markets can coordinate so much? His answer—transaction costs—became foundational. Yet if Coase walked through Amazon's Tilbury fulfilment centre in 2018, watching robotic units allocate tasks and predictive models schedule labour, he might have revised the equation. Coordination, once expensive, now happens at near-zero marginal cost. Something new is doing the work.

The image of a factory driven by three engines—capital, labour, and an emerging algorithmic force—frames this section. It clarifies the puzzle at the heart of contemporary competition: how can a ten-person outfit in Manchester realistically match a national retailer in data-driven decisions? By 2023, a small firm using off-the-shelf forecasting tools from cloud platforms could generate demand predictions, segment customers, and evaluate pricing scenarios in minutes. The models are not bespoke. They are not exclusive. Yet their predictive accuracy rivals what larger firms achieved with entire analytics departments only a decade earlier. Cheap prediction behaves like a quiet third engine, accelerating output without requiring equivalent inputs.

The shift becomes visible when we compare behaviours. A traditional firm decides which products to stock by reviewing past sales, debating intuition, and consulting buyers. The cycle is slow and labour-heavy. A model embedded in the workflow transforms this rhythm: it produces candidate forecasts every night, flags anomalies, recommends quantities, and ranks suppliers. The model does not replace the buyer's judgement; it changes what the buyer sees before deciding. The effect is structural. Once a model supplies continuous prediction at negligible cost, the firm's cost curve bends. Decisions that required meetings, spreadsheets, and negotiation now arrive pre-processed. People commit their attention differently, reserving scarce judgement for ambiguous or strategic choices.

Historical analogies help anchor this shift. When James Watt patented his separate condenser in 1769, the improved steam engine reconfigured the economics of mills. Power became cheap and abundant. Mills migrated from riverbanks to factory towns because capital could now substitute for natural constraints. Today, predictive models substitute for human heuristics in a similar way. They remove bottlenecks in reasoning-intensive tasks. They narrow uncertainty earlier in the process. And, crucially, they run continuously, regardless of firm size. A system that operates 24 hours a day, seven days a week, without fatigue, alters what scale means.

Take Netflix's decision in 2006 to launch the Netflix Prize, offering US$1 million for a measurable improvement to its recommendation algorithm. The competition, run from Los Gatos, California, revealed a truth that remains relevant: improvements in prediction reshape the entire production chain. Better recommendations reduced search time, increased viewing hours, and improved retention. While the company ultimately chose not to deploy the winning model due to engineering constraints, the episode demonstrated the weight an algorithm could exert on costs and customer behaviour. Prediction was not peripheral; it was central to the firm's ability to compete globally.

A contrasting case shows what happens when algorithmic capability outstrips organisational readiness. In 2018, the Australian Government's "Robodebt" programme attempted to automate the detection of welfare overpayments by comparing income records with tax data. The system generated more than 470,000 debt notices, many of them erroneous. The Federal Court later ruled the programme unlawful. The failure illustrated a boundary condition: algorithmic tools are not inherently productive. When deployed without proper domain expertise, safeguards, or human verification, prediction can amplify errors rather than reduce them. The third engine has power, but it is not inherently aligned with accuracy or fairness.

Reconcile these cases and a clearer pattern emerges. Prediction becomes productive only when it is embedded within workflows that treat the model as a disciplined contributor rather than an unquestioned oracle. Productivity gains occur when humans reconfigure their roles to absorb, critique, and refine what the system proposes. Without this integration, the firm gains output but loses coherence.

Return now to the small firm matching its larger rival. The firm's director can use cloud-based demand forecasting to determine stock levels, deploy generative models to draft product descriptions, and rely on automated bidding tools for digital advertising. None of these tools existed at commercial quality ten years earlier. Each of them compresses the time between intent and action. Their cumulative effect is formidable: a firm without a data science team can operate with a degree of informational agility once reserved for corporations with multi-million-pound budgets.

Yet the real competitive shift lies not in raw efficiency but in how decision rights move. When prediction becomes cheap, firms that structure themselves around rapid experimentation gain advantage. A manager who measures the accuracy of a model's forecasts weekly, compares performance across markets, and commits to adjusting strategy based on observed error rates behaves differently from one who treats prediction as an occasional supplement. The former treats the model as a third engine; the latter treats it as a bolt-on. The difference appears in outcomes: inventory turnover improves, markdown rates fall, and product cycles tighten. The structural change is visible in metrics, not rhetoric.

The motif of the third engine reappears here as a diagnostic image. Engines require fuel, maintenance, and clear interfaces. Algorithmic engines require data, feedback loops, and guardrails. They work best when humans know their limits. A forecasting tool cannot interpret a sudden shift in consumer sentiment after a political event. A text-generation model cannot ensure compliance with sector-specific regulations without human review. The engine supplies power, not direction. The exercise of direction remains a human task.

This dynamic reshapes competition. Consider Ocado Technology's 2020 partnership with Kroger in the United States. The collaboration centred on automated fulfilment centres powered by predictive and optimisation models. The technology compressed the distance between order and delivery, forcing competitors to reconsider their cost structures. Retailers that lacked equivalent predictive capability faced a stark choice: invest in similar systems, redesign their operating model, or accept a structural disadvantage. The third engine had altered the competitive baseline.

A limitation tempers the narrative. Prediction is brittle in environments with sparse data or high volatility. The global supply chain disruptions of 2021—partially triggered by pandemic aftershocks and shipping bottlenecks—exposed this brittleness. Models trained on stable patterns faltered. Firms relying solely on algorithmic forecasts faced stock-outs or overordering, while those combining human judgement with model outputs adapted more effectively. The reconciliation lies in complementarity: prediction accelerates routine decisions but cannot fully substitute for strategic sense-making in volatile conditions.

The broader implication for professionals is that economic power now flows not only from capital and labour but from the capacity to *shape* algorithmic engines. Those who define the data, refine the models, and interpret the outputs hold disproportionate influence over outcomes. A firm that treats prediction as infrastructure—not as a project—can reallocate attention to higher-value activities: relationship-building, design, negotiation, and long-range planning. The cost curve bends further when people stop firefighting and start architecting.

Yet the unresolved tension remains. When prediction is cheap and abundant, the constraint shifts from calculation to choice. If a model generates ten viable options for a marketing campaign, which one should a brand pursue? If a system signals twenty potential supply-chain risks, which merit action? If a forecasting engine projects five scenarios with equal probability, which course does a firm commit to?

The third engine produces possibilities. Humans must decide which path to follow.

That leaves a question hanging over the production floor—quiet but insistent. As algorithms take their place alongside capital and labour, who determines which predictions guide the work, and on what terms?

Winners, losers, and leaks

In December 2019, the Court of Appeal in London heard *Uber BV v Aslam*, a case brought by Yaseen Aslam and James Farrar. Both men worked as drivers in the capital and argued that Uber's control over pricing, routing, and performance metrics meant they were workers, not independent contractors. Their claim rested on concrete behaviours: the algorithm decided which journeys they received, how long they waited between fares, and whether they remained on the platform at all. A driver could sit in Islington for twenty minutes, motionless, while the system dictated when they moved next. Human labour was visible; human agency was not. The court ruled in the drivers' favour. The decision, shaped by the invisible logic of a dispatch system built in San Francisco, captured a stark reality: automation redistributes value, but not evenly.

The image of a driver waiting in a parked car will anchor this section. It captures a motif that recurs as automation spreads: stillness at the edge of a system that moves without you. When prediction and coordination migrate to algorithms, the workers who supply physical effort or emotional labour often experience long stretches of passive dependence. They wait, and the system moves. They respond, and the system decides. This quiet asymmetry defines the winners, the losers, and the leaks in automated markets.

To show how value shifts, begin with the most measurable channel: price. Automated systems reduce operational friction. Uber's dispatch engine assigns rides in seconds, reducing idle time; Amazon's fulfilment robots shorten picking cycles, cutting delivery costs; airlines such as British Airways use optimisation models to schedule crews, compressing delays. Lower friction manifests directly in lower prices or faster service. But naming the beneficiaries clarifies the distribution. Consumers gain through cheaper fares or quicker delivery. Firms gain through higher margins. Workers, however, often see little improvement in their unit earnings. In 2017, the UK's Department for Transport found that median hourly pay for private-hire drivers in London had fallen by roughly 8 per cent compared with 2014, a period during which dispatch systems grew markedly more efficient. The efficiency existed. The benefit leaked—towards customers and platforms, not towards those supplying the labour.

A second channel appears in profits. Automated systems scale. Once the model is trained and deployed, the cost of serving an additional user collapses. Spotify's recommendation algorithm, refined after its acquisition of Echo Nest in 2014, guides millions of daily listening decisions with negligible marginal cost. The system's predictions shape what people hear, how long they listen, and whether they remain subscribed. Profits rise as churn falls. The underlying behaviour—listening for longer because the playlist fits your taste—translates directly into retention metrics. Yet the musicians whose songs populate the catalogues face a different calculus. Their per-stream earnings often remain measured in fractions of pennies. The value created by automated curation flows upwards to the platform, not outwards to contributors.

A third channel is time. Automation saves hours, but the question is: for whom? A diagnostic tool in a warehouse might reduce the time engineers spend troubleshooting, freeing them for deeper maintenance. A conversational AI might cut response times in a call centre by producing draft replies. But the distribution of reclaimed time depends on design. If the time saved becomes an opportunity for staff to pursue more meaningful work—training, customer care, system improvement—automation enhances the role. If the time saved becomes an expectation for increased throughput with no additional pay or autonomy, the gain narrows into extraction. The behaviour that signals extraction is simple: tasks increase, but discretion does not.

The rideshare case illustrates these channels simultaneously. Show first. A driver in Manchester opens the app, waits for an alert, accepts a journey, follows the optimised route, and watches their earnings adjust in real time. Surge pricing flickers on and off. Trip length estimates change based on live demand. Every step is shaped by invisible forecasts running on distant servers. Name next. The platform—Uber Technologies Inc.—controls the pricing model, sets the commission structure, measures performance, and can deactivate drivers for low acceptance rates. Explain. Automation coordinates supply and demand with astonishing speed, but the tool's capacity to allocate opportunity and income gives the platform disproportionate power. Algorithmic efficiency increases total rides and reduces passenger waiting time. Yet the driver's hourly earnings remain vulnerable to model updates, market saturation, and incentives designed primarily to shape behaviour rather than reward loyalty. Implication. The system creates winners—passengers and the platform—and partial losers: the drivers whose autonomy shrinks even as demand grows.

To deepen the mapping, add a second named example. Deliveroo, headquartered in London, introduced a free-routing model in 2018 that allowed riders to choose their own paths rather than follow prescribed routes. The change appeared to grant autonomy. But internal data showed that riders who deviated from algorithmic suggestions often earned less per hour because the model had already calculated the optimal sequence of drops. Riders gained choice but lost income unless they conformed to the model's predictions. Autonomy and earnings diverged. The behavioural signal was clear: independence existed on screen, not in practice.

A counter-example grounds the analysis. The Finnish postal service, Posti, tested automated sorting systems in Helsinki in 2017. Rather than displacing workers or narrowing their roles, Posti reconfigured shifts to allow staff to rotate between machine-supervised tasks and customer-facing services. The automation reduced repetitive strain injuries and created a blended role that staff reported as more fulfilling (Posti internal report, 2018). The system offered efficiency without stripping agency. Limitation acknowledged; reconciliation follows. Automation does not dictate uneven value capture. Design choices do. The distribution of benefits is not technologically fixed; it is organisationally constructed.

Consider why value leaks at all. First, algorithms favour scale. A model that improves prediction accuracy by 3 per cent yields enormous returns when applied across millions of transactions. A driver or warehouse worker cannot multiply their hours in the same way. The returns pool where the scaling occurs. Second, algorithms create switching costs. A passenger accustomed to seamless app-based travel rarely compares alternatives; the platform retains their custom. Workers, by contrast, often face fragmented labour markets. Third, algorithmic opacity makes negotiation difficult. A driver cannot contest a fare calculation they cannot see. A warehouse operative cannot evaluate the fairness of task allocation if the optimisation model is proprietary. Lack of visibility reduces bargaining power.

A fourth factor is the quiet motif that threads through this piece: the system's *centre of gravity*. In automated markets, the centre of gravity often rests within the model. The system anticipates demand, allocates supply, sequences tasks, and evaluates performance. Human contributors orbit this centre. Some orbits are stable—engineers who design, test, and refine the model gain influence. Others are precarious—front-line workers whose roles are fragmented into micro-tasks lose continuity. When the centre of gravity is opaque, power concentrates.

Trace that concentration in concrete behaviours. A driver accepts a far-off trip because declining might reduce their "utilisation score" and risk deactivation. A restaurant accepts a lower commission from a delivery platform because the algorithmic ranking determines visibility on the app. A warehouse worker races to meet a target set not by a manager but by a machine-calculated benchmark based on average picking speed. Each behaviour signals the same dynamic: the system's model evaluates them, not the other way around.

Yet concentration is not inevitable. Rules and design can counter it, redistributing value through transparency and constraint. The *Uber BV v Aslam* ruling imposed statutory rights—minimum wage, rest breaks, holiday pay—based on the reality of algorithmic control. Regulation shifted the balance, making the benefits of automation spill more equitably across the chain. Similar moves appear elsewhere. In 2021, the European Commission proposed the *Platform*

Work Directive, aiming to clarify algorithmic management practices and grant workers access to meaningful explanation of automated decisions. Such rules offer guardrails for the centre of gravity: they limit how far power can drift.

Design also reshapes who wins. A firm that publishes clear criteria for how its task-allocation model works invites scrutiny. A platform that lets workers view performance metrics and contest anomalies distributes informational power. Concrete design choices—explainable dashboards, audit trails, override rights—anchor agency. They slow the drift towards concentration. They turn the opaque centre of gravity into a shared reference point.

The deeper implication is that automation generates winners, losers, and leaks through *architecture*, not merely code. Who captures value depends on whose priorities the model encodes, whose behaviour it measures, and whose outcomes it optimises. If the model optimises for speed alone, workers absorb pressure. If it optimises for long-term reliability, tasks and incentives shift differently. The question is not whether automation creates efficiency, but who stands closest to the spigot.

As we reach the edge of this subchapter, the parked car returns as motif. The driver waits for the next alert. The algorithm hums. Passengers move freely. Value circulates, but not evenly. One unresolved question remains, quiet yet decisive: when automated systems coordinate the market, who decides where the value should settle—and on what grounds?

Defining human advantage

In October 2022, at The Ledbury in Notting Hill, head chef Brett Graham tested a new experiment. He asked his team to feed an AI-based recipe generator with the restaurant's archive of menus—years' worth of venison preparations, ferment notes, and seasonal pairings. The model produced dozens of combinations overnight. Some were uncanny, some pedestrian, some unusable. One suggestion, a pairing of smoked beetroot and aged pigeon with a juniper glaze, looked promising on screen but collapsed in the pan. Graham kept one idea only: a salt-aged carrot reduction the model paired with fermented grains. The dish that reached diners bore almost no resemblance to the generated recipe. It carried his touch: restrained, balanced, and steeped in the restaurant's philosophy. The machine had produced raw material. Graham decided what mattered. His menu affirmed a principle quietly shaping this chapter: judgement sits above generation.

The kitchen scene illuminates a wider shift. Systems can produce thousands of options—menus, marketing lines, design sketches—yet the act of choosing the right one remains acutely human. A model generates a list; a chef discards nine-tenths of it. A system drafts an email; a manager reshapes the tone. These micro-decisions reflect a deeper asymmetry: abundance is automated, but meaning is curated. The tension between what machines propose and what humans accept is the space in which capability forms. It is also the space in which advantage endures.

Human advantage rests on four scarce capacities: framing problems, exercising taste, applying ethical judgement, and building relationships. Each capacity manifests in visible behaviour—where attention goes, which choices are made, which stories are told—and each resists full automation because it requires context no dataset can fully encode.

Begin with framing. Show first. In 2020, during the early months of the pandemic, researchers at University College London worked with NHS clinicians to build triage support tools. The models predicted probable outcomes based on patient data from specific London hospitals. Their accuracy was reasonable, but their usefulness depended entirely on how clinicians framed the problem: was the goal to reduce ICU load, minimise mortality, or prioritise certain risk groups? Name next. Dr. Natalie Silvey, one of the medical leads, insisted that no model could decide the *purpose* of triage. Explain. The frame—what counts as success—shaped every subsequent decision: which features mattered, which outcomes were acceptable, which trade-offs were ethically defensible. The model computed probabilities; clinicians defined the problem. Implication. Framing is not clerical. It is an act of interpretation that governs everything downstream. A system cannot supply it because it requires consensus, values, and contextual judgement.

Taste forms the second scarcity. It is a capacity often minimised because it appears subjective. Yet taste is measurable. It shows up in what people keep returning to—restaurants with waiting lists, magazines with enduring influence, designs that gather awards. The chef at The Ledbury did not simply assess the AI's suggestions; he compared them to a mental library of textures, temperatures, and memories. That comparison is relational. It draws on sensory history and cultural fluency. A machine can mimic patterns, but it cannot hold an atmosphere in mind. To name this dynamic more formally, psychologist Daniel Kahneman (2011) distinguished between fast pattern recognition and slow, reflective evaluation. Models excel at the former; taste requires the latter. When a designer in Edinburgh selects one logo among fifty AI-generated variants, the choice reflects coherence with brand story, audience sensibility, and the designer's personal sense of restraint. The implication is simple and sharp: abundance amplifies the value of discernment.

Ethical judgement forms the third human advantage. Show. In April 2018, the Swedish Transport Agency released an audit revealing that automated decision systems used in migrant processing produced inconsistent assessments for similar cases. Caseworkers had relied on the system's scores without adequately challenging anomalies. Name. Legal scholar Mireille Hildebrandt has written extensively on "computational normativity", warning that models encode assumptions invisible to citizens (2016). Explain. Ethical judgement requires recognising when a model's output may conflict with fairness, dignity, or due process. This recognition is behavioural, not theoretical. It appears when a caseworker pauses and requests additional context, or when a manager refuses to automate an edge case because harm outweighs speed. Implication. Ethics is a practice of refusal as much as action. Machines cannot refuse for moral reasons. They can only return outputs.

The fourth capacity—relationship-building—resists automation because it depends on reciprocity. Show. In 2019, a study of oncology consultations at the University of Cambridge found that patient trust increased when clinicians acknowledged uncertainty explicitly. Naming uncertainty reduced anxiety. The behaviour—pausing, making eye contact, explaining risk—cannot be automated because it is relational, not procedural. A generative model can draft empathetic phrases; it cannot engender trust without a human presence committing to care. Relationships bloom from embodied signals: slowed speech, shared humour, the willingness to stay in the room when conversations turn difficult. Machines cannot perform vulnerability.

Two more named examples clarify these capacities and tie them to concrete outcomes. In 2021, the Rijksmuseum in Amsterdam used machine-learning tools to reconstruct missing parts of Rembrandt's *The Night Watch*. The model generated plausible brushstrokes by analysing thousands of high-resolution scans. Yet the curators rejected several outputs because they "felt un-Rembrandt-like". The measure of authenticity came not from the model's probability score but from curatorial judgement grounded in decades of training. The visible behaviour—rejecting a technically competent output because it lacked artistic truth—shows taste in action.

A second example comes from the world of sport. In 2020, Liverpool FC's analytics department used predictive models to scout talent. The models highlighted players with unusually high "packing rates"—passes that bypass multiple opponents. Yet the final decision to sign a player still rested with human scouts. They watched behaviour under pressure, noted body language during setbacks, and assessed team fit. These dimensions appear nowhere in the data. The implication is consistent: prediction can spotlight potential; judgement decides significance.

A counter-example reveals the limits of asserting human superiority without nuance. In 2022, Google DeepMind's AlphaFold system achieved remarkable accuracy in predicting protein structures—a task that previously consumed months of human effort. The achievement demonstrated that some cognitive activities once thought deeply intuitive can be partially automated. Reconcile this with human advantage by noting that AlphaFold solved a bounded, highly formalised problem with clear ground truth. Framing, taste, ethics, and relationships do not share that boundedness. They evolve with context. They require meaning, not only pattern. The human edge lies not in raw cognition but in the capacity to interpret, prioritise, and commit under ambiguity.

Thread the quiet motif now: the menu. In high-end restaurants, the menu is a system of decisions. It reflects what the kitchen believes is worth presenting, what the season supports, what the diners will understand, and what story the restaurant wishes to tell. The AI can generate a dish. It cannot compose a menu. The act of curation—deciding what fits, what clashes, what honours the restaurant's identity—encapsulates the four human scarcities. Framing sets the narrative arc of the meal. Taste selects the best from the possible. Ethics governs sourcing. Relationships animate service.

The motif extends beyond food. A teacher adapts a lesson because a pupil looks confused. A journalist changes the angle of a story after sensing public mood. A manager reorders priorities after a tense meeting reveals unspoken conflict. In each case, the behaviour—adjusting course based on subtle cues—signals judgement. Machines lack those cues because they lack lived experience.

Human advantage persists not because machines are weak, but because humans hold responsibility. Framing requires committing to a path. Taste requires risking failure. Ethics requires drawing a line. Relationships require showing up. These acts carry weight. They demand presence. They ask something of us that cannot be delegated.

As we approach the end of this subchapter, the kitchen returns. The chef reviews another batch of model-generated recipes. The screen glows. Possible dishes crowd the interface. He scrolls, considers, discards. Then he pauses on one idea—not because the model rated it highly, but because it sparks something: a memory, a season, a story he wants to tell. He sketches the dish on a notepad. He tests it. He adjusts acidity. He tastes again.

One question remains, hanging like the scent of roasted herbs over the pass: when the machine can propose everything, what will you choose to make—and why?

Chapter 2
Skills That Compound

The mistakes were small at first—an overlooked dependency, a vague specification, a user flow that collapsed under real-world pressure. Nothing catastrophic, just the quiet errors that accumulate in the margins of complex work. The product manager responsible, a steady and thoughtful colleague named Leila, had seen these missteps before. Each one looked trivial; together they created a pattern. Deadlines slipped. Stakeholders fretted. The team lost confidence. Then, midway through a fraught launch cycle, she tried something new. Before the next release, she drafted a set of "red-team prompts"—pointed questions designed to imagine failure in advance, like: "What would break first if the forecast is wrong?" "Which assumption depends on a user behaving perfectly?" "Where are we extrapolating from too little data?" The exercise took less than an hour. It halved the next round of launch issues. Two cycles later, launch defects were down by nearly 70 per cent. Nothing magical had happened. She had simply improved her judgement—deliberately, repeatedly—until it became a force multiplier. Small inputs. Large returns. That is the essence of a compounding skill.

We live in a world flooded with information yet starved of discernment. The paradox is everywhere. Teams have dashboards but not clarity. They have templates but not coherence. They have data but not insight. Knowledge has become abundant to the point of saturation. Judgement, by contrast, remains stubbornly scarce. And scarcity, as every serious reader knows, is a signal of value. What separates the merely competent from the quietly exceptional is not what they know, but how they decide.

This chapter begins with that distinction because the stakes are high. In the preceding pages, automation blurred the boundary between human and machine capability. Systems generate options at industrial scale: hundreds of design variants, dozens of product concepts, infinite lines of code or prose. Yet choosing well—framing, prioritising, discerning, negotiating—remains resolutely human. When everything is possible, the scarce skill becomes knowing what is worth doing. The terrain of work is shifting fast; the anchor points are shifting slowly. This is the chapter about those anchor points.

Judgement is the first and most foundational. It grows through practice, not prestige. Techniques such as pre-mortems, checklists, and calibration sound prosaic until you watch how they transform the rhythm of work. A pre-mortem reframes the future: "Assume failure happened—what caused it?" A checklist reduces error by making the invisible visible. Calibration builds the discipline of estimating your own uncertainty. These are not rituals of caution; they are rituals of foresight. They help you see around corners. And because they can be repeated weekly, even daily, the benefits compound like interest accumulating quietly in the background.

Taste comes next—perhaps the most misunderstood skill in modern work. It is often reduced to preference, as though selecting the right design, headline, or strategy were a matter of whim. But taste is not whim. Taste is the disciplined ability to recognise which option carries narrative coherence, emotional truth, or conceptual integrity. To watch a designer at work is to see this distinction made tangible. One example: a designer in Glasgow iterates dozens of logo concepts with an AI model, each variant technically plausible. But the chosen mark—the one that survives critique and rounds of refinement—is the one that fits the brand's story like a key sliding into a lock. The machine produced fragments; the human made meaning. Taste is the skill that turns abundance into identity.

Relationship work follows—a skill so deeply human that attempts to automate it reveal its boundaries with almost comic clarity. Trust emerges from repeated signals of reliability: replying when it matters, showing understanding in tense moments, naming conflict before it festers. Negotiation arises from shared context: knowing when to soften a stance or when to hold firm. Meaning arises from ongoing dialogue: the micro-adjustments people make to stay aligned. No system performs these acts with credibility because they depend on embodied attention—the kind that notices hesitation in a colleague's voice or a flicker of doubt in their posture. Watch a nurse coordinating care on a busy ward with assistance from decision-support software. The machine provides risk scores. The nurse provides reassurance. The machine recommends interventions. The nurse senses which family member needs an extra minute of explanation. Empathy stabilises the system. Without it, the best predictions ring hollow.

Then there is learning—not the episodic learning of courses and workshops, but the slow, steady kind that accrues through a deliberate rhythm of scanning, practising, shipping, and reflecting. The 90-minute weekly cycle proposed in this chapter is deceptively simple: gather exposure to new ideas, try one technique in a low-stakes environment, release something tangible, and analyse the gap between expectation and outcome. A sales representative in Leeds used this rhythm with a prompt library, running micro-experiments every Thursday morning. After six weeks, her outreach hit-rates doubled. After twelve, she began contributing improvements to the team's workflow. She did not reinvent herself. She simply created conditions for compounding.

What binds these skills together—judgement, taste, relationship work, learning—is that none of them depend on raw knowledge. They depend on refinement: the sharpening of attention, the cultivation of pattern awareness, the sensitivity to context, the ability to match intention to action. In fields overwhelmed by automation, where models and tools proliferate faster than any human could hope to master, these skills are the constants. They resist obsolescence precisely because they adapt. They are not technical; they are developmental.

The significance becomes clearer when we consider a quiet motif running through this chapter: the idea of *distillation*. In every example, the human contributor is distilling something—options into strategy, signals into meaning, experiences into judgement. Distillation requires constraint. It requires choosing what to ignore as much as what to pursue. Machines excel at expansion; humans excel at compression. That asymmetry is unlikely to change.

Yet cultivating these skills demands more than technique. It requires a certain orientation to work. One that prizes depth over breadth. One that rewards consistency over intensity. One that recognises that compounding occurs not through the occasional breakthrough but through the habitual, almost mundane, act of improving the smallest unit of practice. A pre-mortem becomes instinct. A reference library becomes a source of creative gravity. A stakeholder map becomes a living document. A weekly experiment becomes a ritual of progress. The transformation is cumulative. Within months, your thinking sharpens; within years, the difference is unmistakable.

The automation age makes this orientation urgent. When tools generate plausible output with ease, inadequacy hides behind competence. You can appear skilled without being so. You can produce work that is smooth yet hollow. The distinction between signal and noise shifts from production to selection. It is your judgement, not your typing speed;

your taste, not your prompt; your relationships, not your templates; your learning rhythm, not your course certificates, that determine the value of your contribution. Quality becomes a function of discernment.

The chapter ahead will map these skills with the same care used to map a new terrain. Each section offers a route into a capability that matures over time. Each one shows how small acts compound. The stories—from Leila's product launches to the designer's curated marks to the nurse's stabilising presence to the sales representative's weekly experiments—anchor the methods in lived experience. But the deeper purpose is not merely to teach techniques. It is to shift the reader's sense of what mastery looks like in an age that confuses information with intelligence.

We are entering a period in which the rarest individuals will be those who can combine these skills with intention. People who make better decisions because they question themselves rigorously. People who create resonant work because they cultivate references deliberately. People who build durable trust because they read emotional landscapes with clarity. People who evolve continuously because they embed learning into the grain of their week. They will not be the loudest voices. They will be the most effective ones.

As this introduction draws to a close, the chapter opens like a doorway. It offers a path anchored in skills that endure, deepen, and amplify one another. It speaks to the reader not as a passive recipient of change but as an active architect of capability. Ahead lie practical methods, vivid cases, and intellectual frameworks designed to reshape how you develop yourself.

But one question must accompany you as you step forward: if machines can generate competence, what skill—practised repeatedly, refined carefully—will make you unmistakably distinct?

Judgement over knowledge

In March 2020, as London offices emptied and product teams scattered to their spare rooms and kitchen tables, a product manager at Monzo Bank named Leila Fidler faced a problem she could measure. Her team's latest feature—an automated budgeting tool—had launched with eight separate defects despite months of preparation. The errors ranged from an overlooked permissions model to an incompatibility affecting roughly 4,200 users. None caused catastrophic harm, but together they formed a pattern: the team knew a great deal, yet they were deciding poorly. Two cycles later, Fidler tried something unusual. She introduced a set of "red-team prompts" before every release. The questions were blunt, specific, and sceptical: *Where is the assumption with the highest blast radius? Which user segment behaves least like our personas? What breaks first under stress?* Within a quarter, launch issues had fallen by half. What changed was not knowledge. What changed was judgement.

This distinction—between what a team knows and how a team decides—has become one of the defining lines of modern work. Knowledge has never been cheaper. It pours into dashboards, models, and documents at a rate no professional can keep up with. Yet judgement, the ability to interpret context, weigh trade-offs, and anticipate failure, remains scarce. The scarcity is visible in the workplace behaviours that matter most: which risks teams spot early, which issues they ignore, which opportunities they pursue, and which they let pass unnoticed. A quiet motif emerges here, one we will return to: the unanswered question. Good judgement grows from asking the right questions before events force the answers upon you.

Begin with the first principle: knowledge often obscures judgement rather than strengthening it. Show first. In 2011, the Fukushima Daiichi nuclear plant in Japan experienced a cascading failure after a tsunami overtopped its sea walls. The inquiry that followed revealed no shortage of technical expertise; the engineering teams had decades of collective knowledge. Name next. The Diet of Japan's 2012 investigation concluded that the disaster reflected a "failure of imagination" more than a failure of data. Explain. The engineers had accurate models of earthquake risk, but they had not engaged in structured exercises to imagine how those models might be wrong. Implication. Information did not fail them. Judgement did—the kind that anticipates improbable but consequential scenarios.

Techniques such as pre-mortems exist to correct this imbalance. A pre-mortem asks a team to assume that failure has already happened, then explain why. The behaviour it produces is concrete: teams name weak assumptions, identify neglected dependencies, and surface silent disagreements. The effect is immediate. It forces attention towards the flanks rather than the familiar centre. When Fidler introduced red-team prompts, she was, in essence, operationalising a pre-mortem. The prompts disciplined the team to think like adversaries rather than advocates, collapsing blind spots that would otherwise have matured into defects.

Checklists form the second technique, and their seriousness is often underestimated. Show. In 2009, the World Health Organisation published the results of its Surgical Safety Checklist trial across eight hospitals—from Toronto to Amman. After implementation, major complications fell from 11 per cent to 7 per cent; mortality dropped from 1.5 per cent to 0.8 per cent (WHO, 2009). Name next. Atul Gawande, the surgeon behind much of the checklist's design, emphasised that its power lay not in its items but in its enforcement of disciplined attention. Explain. A checklist shifts the cognitive burden: instead of relying on memory, practitioners rely on process. It turns judgement from an improvisational act into a repeatable one. Implication. When stakes are high and information abundant, a checklist preserves bandwidth for decisions that cannot be scripted.

Calibration completes the triad. Calibration is the skill of knowing how confident to be. It appears in visible, measurable behaviours: estimating a probability, recording the outcome, comparing the two. Show. Since 2017, the

"Good Judgment Project" has trained forecasters to improve their predictive accuracy by practising calibration on geopolitical events. Participants learn to adjust their confidence levels based on feedback, gradually tightening the gap between expectation and reality. Name next. Psychologist Philip Tetlock, co-founder of the project, demonstrated that well-calibrated forecasters outperform intelligence analysts with privileged information (Tetlock & Gardner, 2015). Explain. Calibration teaches humility without paralysis; it trains professionals to distinguish what they know from what they assume. Implication. Organisations that cultivate calibration make better strategic decisions because they reward accuracy, not bravado.

The absence of judgement is most visible where systems automate the hard parts of knowledge but leave the hard parts of decision-making untouched. Contrast two examples. First, in 2018, the UK's National Audit Office reviewed the Home Office's automated visa-processing system. The system flagged anomalies efficiently, yet staff routinely accepted its scores without interrogating edge cases. Errors compounded. The visible behaviour was unquestioned acceptance: staff clicked "approve" because the model suggested it. Judgement evaporated. Next, consider a counter-example: in 2021, the Danish Medicines Agency used machine-learning models to triage pharmacovigilance reports. Staff reviewed each flagged case manually, challenging model outputs whenever clinical intuition suggested nuance. The result was a faster, safer triage process. Reconcile the two. Automation strengthens decision-making only where judgement interrogates it; without interrogation, it amplifies error.

This dynamic returns us to Fidler at Monzo and the quiet motif of the unanswered question. Her red-team prompts created deliberate friction. They forced the team to confront their assumptions early rather than late. The behaviour changed: engineers proposed alternative flows; designers flagged usability gaps before development; analysts re-tested their baseline metrics. The rhythm of meetings shifted from presentation to scrutiny. Judgement compounded.

But judgement expands beyond rituals. It begins with framing—deciding what the real problem is. Consider a second named example. In 2015, Rolls-Royce undertook an internal review of its aircraft engine monitoring systems. Engineers in Derby monitored thousands of signals per engine: temperature, vibration, fuel flow. Yet incident reports still surprised teams. The review found that although engineers were swimming in data, they lacked clarity about which anomalies were mission-critical. They reframed the problem. Instead of analysing every signal equally, they curated a smaller set of indicators tied to safety margins. Judgement improved not from more knowledge but from better framing. Decisions accelerated.

Now introduce a limitation: judgement can be trained, but not fully standardised. People vary in temperament. Some shy from uncertainty; some rush into it. A firm in Sydney attempted in 2020 to roll out a company-wide calibration programme for risk assessments. The effort underperformed. Staff treated the exercises as compliance tasks, not developmental ones. Numbers improved on paper but not in practice. How to reconcile this? Judgement improves only when individuals commit to the discomfort of acknowledging uncertainty. Techniques can guide, but cannot replace the willingness to be wrong publicly and repeatedly.

The motif of unanswered questions appears again. Good judgement is not the elimination of uncertainty; it is the capacity to live with uncertainty while making commitments. It is visible in the product manager who asks, *What's the failure we haven't imagined?* It is visible in the surgeon who pauses to read the checklist aloud. It is visible in the engineer who recalibrates a probability after re-examining evidence. Knowledge supports these acts; it does not perform them.

A deeper implication emerges. In a world where automated systems generate plausible options instantly, the bottleneck shifts from access to interpretation. The individual with the best search tools is no longer the most capable. The individual with the best judgement is. Because judgement compounds, even small improvements in how a person anticipates failure, frames problems, and calibrates confidence accumulate across months and years. The returns become structural: fewer crises, cleaner launches, quieter teams, clearer choices.

As this subchapter approaches its final movement, the scene returns to Fidler at her kitchen table. Another release nears. Another set of prompts waits on her screen. She scans the questions. She pauses. She adjusts one prompt to reflect a new dependency discovered that morning. She sends the document to her team with a brief note: *"If we had to explain a post-mortem tomorrow, what would embarrass us today?"* The question hangs in the air. It sharpens attention. It focuses minds.

One unresolved tension follows, inevitable and instructive: when every tool can supply information instantly, what will ensure that your next decision reflects judgement rather than noise?

Taste and editorial sense

In July 2014, in a conference room at Airbnb's headquarters in San Francisco, the design agency DesignStudio presented the company with a new logo and visual system. The proposed mark, later called the "Bélo", was controversial from the moment it appeared on screen. Internally, though, the debate was less about geometry and more about story: did this symbol carry the company's narrative of "belonging anywhere" without collapsing into generic travel branding? The team had reviewed hundreds of sketches and routes, more than enough "adequate options" for a fast-growing platform. Yet they chose one design, and one only. Not because it was objectively perfect, but because it aligned with a carefully built reference of icons, narratives, and emotional cues. Taste did something different. It selected, refined, and committed.

That decision was not an act of whimsy. It rested on years of accumulated visual memory: notes from user research, screenshots of competitor brands, photographs of host homes, and sketches pinned to studio walls. The designers and executives did not simply ask, "Do we like it?" They asked, "Does this feel like us? Will it still feel like us when we double in size? Will it work in Tokyo and Toulouse?" Behind each question sat a mental library of examples. The choice reflected something subtle yet decisive: an editorial sense capable of navigating abundance.

Automation has intensified this abundance. A designer sitting in Glasgow, working on a logo for a local co-operative in 2023, can generate a hundred plausible marks in minutes using AI-based image tools. All of them "work" at a superficial level. They have symmetry, legible typography, on-trend colour palettes. Yet only a handful will carry the co-op's story about shared ownership, trust, and locality. The crucial act is not producing options; it is curating the few that deserve to exist. In a world where generation is cheap, taste becomes an economic function.

Taste is frequently misunderstood as mere preference, a question of personal liking. But in the context of work, taste is better understood as disciplined discrimination: the ability to recognise which option fits a narrative, a context, and a future. Show, name, explain, implication. Show: a designer moves a logo two millimetres and removes a secondary colour. Name: they say, "The mark breathes better now; the supporting colour was shouting." Explain: the adjustment increases legibility at small sizes and matches the brand's restrained tone. Implication: the logo survives on a phone screen in Nairobi and a billboard in Newcastle. Taste, here, is not an aesthetic luxury. It is a prediction about real-world performance.

This disciplined discrimination rests on reference. Designers, editors, and product leaders who make consistently strong choices tend to maintain some form of reference library. Historically, that library took physical form: shelves of magazines, drawers of tear-sheets, folders of photos. Now it might live in Figma boards, Pinterest collections, or local folders of screenshots. The specific medium matters less than the behaviour: regular collection, periodic review, and critical comparison. The reference library becomes a quiet motif—a wall, physical or digital, against which each new option is tested.

This is how taste is taught within serious creative practices. At Pentagram's London office, for example, junior designers sit through critiques where partners such as Harry Pearce or Marina Willer do something deceptively simple: they place a new design next to a historically strong reference and talk through the differences. Not "I like it" or "I don't like it", but "This one collapses at distance", "This loses its character when reversed", "This misreads in Arabic". They tie aesthetic judgement to observable behaviour: how the mark survives reproduction, how it reads across cultures, how it behaves in motion. Over time, juniors internalise this structure. Their taste matures not as a set of likes, but as a set of tested principles.

The presence of AI tools makes this process both easier and more necessary. Easier, because reference material can be generated on demand. A designer exploring a symbol for a climate charity can prompt an image model with "global solidarity, non-corporate, hopeful" and receive visual suggestions that might not have emerged from their own hand. More necessary, because these suggestions arrive without context or constraint. A system cannot know that the charity wishes to avoid leaf motifs because they are overused, or that certain colours carry political associations in particular countries. The human must bring that context to bear.

Here the motif of the wall returns. Imagine a digital board split into three columns: "interesting", "strong", "ours". In the first column sit raw AI outputs, collected quickly. In the second, a smaller set refined by critique: legibility at different sizes, colour contrast scores, tests against accessibility guidelines. In the third, perhaps one or two options only, chosen because they resonate with the organisation's story, values, and future ambitions. The movement from column to column is editorial work. It requires saying no far more often than yes.

Taste is not confined to visual design. Editorial sense shows up whenever someone chooses which ideas deserve attention. In 2019, the Financial Times in London reported that its data desk received far more story leads from algorithms than journalists could possibly chase. The editorial team did not celebrate the volume. Instead, they built filters: criteria that prioritised stories with structural significance over those likely to generate short-term clicks. The behaviour here is specific: stories that merely spiked page views were often declined in favour of those that explained underlying shifts in trade, policy, or corporate power. The implication is important. Taste directs institutional energy. It can keep a newsroom from becoming an automated reaction engine.

A counter-example shows what happens when taste is weak or absent. In October 2010, Gap unveiled a redesigned logo, replacing its familiar navy box with a lighter, more minimal mark. The company had access to extensive consumer research and creative options. Yet the final choice felt characterless. Public reaction was swift and negative. Within a week, Gap reverted to its original logo. What failed was not access to visual possibilities but the editorial judgement that selects an option with narrative continuity. The logo did not feel like an evolution of Gap's identity; it felt like an arbitrary swap. The wall of references, if it existed, had not been used rigorously.

Reconcile this with the success of the Airbnb redesign, which also attracted criticism but endured. The difference lies in how deeply each organisation tied the mark to its broader narrative. Airbnb's Bélo appeared consistently across product interfaces, host materials, and experiential design. It was accompanied by a story about belonging, told repeatedly. Gap's short-lived logo, by contrast, appeared as a surface-level tweak, unmoored from a larger vision. Taste, then, is not only about choosing a symbol; it is about committing to its story and executing it through time.

That time dimension matters, particularly in an automation-rich environment. AI tools are good at producing what is currently fashionable. Prompt a model for "modern tech logo" and it will dutifully assemble gradients, rounded sans-serifs, and abstract glyphs reminiscent of existing brands. If a team chases this output uncritically, their visual identity will age as quickly as the trend cycle. Taste resists this pull. It asks, "Will this still feel credible in five years?" and checks against a reference library that includes work with enduring strength. The visible behaviour is chronological comparison: placing a new identity next to a mark from 1990 that still works, and asking whether the new work has similar resilience.

Critique is the engine of this maturation. Not vague commentary, but structured dialogue. In well-run design studios, critique sessions follow a pattern. The presenter explains the brief in one or two sentences—enough to anchor discussion. Colleagues respond with observations tied to outcomes: "This version reads more clearly at 16 pixels", "The spacing here suggests luxury, but the product is mass-market", "The colour shift improves contrast for colour-blind users". Even when courteous, the tone is exacting. Ideas are separated from egos. The metric is fitness-for-purpose, not personal attachment. Over time, participants learn to run a version of this critique internally. They replay the questions while working alone. That internalised voice is editorial sense.

The designer working with AI-generated logos can harness this habit. Rather than asking, "Which one looks best?", they might ask, "Which three marks differ meaningfully in concept?", "How does each behave in monochrome?", "What story does each suggest about the organisation's character?" The questions force structural comparison rather than vague preference. They transform the AI tool into a generator of raw clay, shaped by human hands.

Taste also has an ethical dimension. Editorial decisions can protect or harm. In 2018, YouTube's recommendation algorithm came under scrutiny for promoting sensational and conspiratorial content because such material drove watch time. The absence here was editorial sense at scale: a willingness to override purely behavioural metrics in favour of societal impact. Some news organisations responded by building their own curated playlists and channels, manually selecting videos aligned with editorial standards. The behaviour—choosing not to amplify certain content despite its popularity—illustrates taste as restraint. Automation expands; taste restricts. That restriction carries moral weight.

There is a limitation worth acknowledging. Taste can be exclusionary when left unexamined. A reference library composed only of Western brands will bias decisions in predictable ways. A critique culture that equates "polished" with "professional" may marginalise vernacular design that resonates more deeply with particular communities. To reconcile this, serious practitioners deliberately diversify their references. They add posters from Lagos, book covers from São Paulo, signage from Seoul. They invite critique from people outside their usual circle. The wall enlarges. Taste becomes less about enforcing a narrow ideal and more about recognising coherence within a broader field.

The motif of the wall returns one last time. Imagine walking past your own reference wall—physical or digital. What does it contain? Which patterns recur? Which gaps glare back? In an age of abundant, automated options, that wall is not decorative. It is the infrastructure of your decisions.

A designer scanning dozens of AI-generated logos for a small co-operative eventually drags one mark into the "ours" column. It is not objectively the most intricate or on-trend. But it carries something the others lack: the hint of a story the co-op actually lives. She circles it in red on the board. She deletes the rest.

A question follows, quiet but insistent: when a machine can produce endless adequate options on command, what, exactly, will you teach your eye—and your organisation—to recognise as worth keeping?

Relationship work

In February 2017, at Salford Royal NHS Foundation Trust in Greater Manchester, a senior nurse named Fiona Mitchell began a morning shift on Ward H4 with the support of an electronic decision-support system newly deployed across the hospital. The software surfaced risk scores, flagged early signs of deterioration, and suggested monitoring intervals for each patient. Yet the decisive moments of Fiona's shift were not generated by the system. They occurred in the gaps between its prompts: a quiet explanation to a worried daughter, a tactful negotiation with a junior doctor about reprioritising a medication round, a gentle but firm conversation with a porter whose timetable conflicted with a patient transfer. By noon, the system had processed hundreds of data points. Fiona had mediated half a dozen small tensions that kept the ward flowing. Her empathy stabilised a complex environment that did not run on data alone. In the language of this chapter, she was practising relationship work: the craft of trust, negotiation, and shared meaning.

The scene at Salford Royal shows something essential that automation cannot touch. Trust emerges from observable behaviour—how someone explains uncertainty, how consistently they follow through, how they respond when things go wrong. Negotiation unfolds through tone, posture, and timing, not simply through information exchange. Shared meaning arises from the willingness to interpret another's perspective generously, especially when stakes diverge. These are not abstractions. They manifest in specific actions, like Fiona sitting on the edge of a patient's bed to lower the emotional temperature, or pausing to ask a colleague, "What matters most to you in this decision?" No model can reconstruct those acts from data alone because their power lies in context, presence, and relational attunement.

Automation thrives on prediction and repetition; relationships thrive on responsiveness. Show, name, explain, implication. Show: a nurse reads a risk alert but notices a patient's hesitation before answering a question. Name: she treats the hesitation as information not reflected in the alert. Explain: the blend of clinical insight and interpersonal awareness produces a safer plan of care. Implication: the system performs better because a human interprets its outputs through a social lens. Relationship work strengthens the work of machines without mimicking it.

The same logic plays out in corporate settings. In 2015, Rolls-Royce in Derby undertook a redesign of its engineering review process for long-term engine service agreements. Data models could forecast component wear and suggest maintenance intervals with growing accuracy. Yet one of the senior programme leads, David Joyce, noticed that disagreements between engineering, finance, and customer teams repeatedly caused delays. The numbers were solid; the relationships were brittle. Joyce instituted structured cross-discipline conversations, using simple scripts such as, "State your concern in one sentence; state your assumption in one more." The behaviour changed. Disputes shrank from weeks to hours. People discovered that misalignment stemmed more from interpretation than from analysis. Relationship work resolved what models could only illuminate.

Stakeholder mapping makes this visible. It is a technique that charts interests, influence, alliances, and fault lines. But the map becomes meaningful only when animated through conversation. A project manager at the BBC in 2019 used a standard power-interest grid during the rollout of a new internal publishing tool. The grid revealed that a small, overstretched editorial team held high influence but low bandwidth. Rather than pushing a technical deadline, the manager scheduled a series of short, respectful consultations, asking, "What would make this easier for you?" The tension eased. Adoption accelerated. Again, the pattern is clear: relational choices altered the outcome more than technical ones.

A counter-example sharpens the argument. In 2020, a large UK retailer attempted to automate frontline conflict resolution through scripted customer-service chatbots. The system could escalate issues based on sentiment analysis, but it frequently misread emotional nuance. One incident involved a customer grieving the loss of a parent; the chatbot offered a discount code. Complaints surged. Staff had to repair trust through long phone calls, offering human presence where automation had bluntly failed. The limitation is obvious: relationship work is not transcription. It is interpretation, timing, and care. You cannot automate sincerity.

Reconcile this with the growing use of AI in high-pressure environments, such as emergency departments using triage algorithms or banks using automated fraud alerts. These systems excel at surfacing patterns early. They are tools for vigilance. Yet their outputs often require delicate framing. A fraud alert delivered without explanation can damage customer confidence. A triage warning delivered mechanically can trigger unnecessary alarm. Humans modulate. They choose words carefully. They decide when to soften, when to clarify, when to pause. Relationship work sits precisely at this intersection—where information becomes communication and communication becomes trust.

The quiet motif that threads through this subchapter is the handover. In complex systems—hospitals, aviation, logistics, software operations—the handover is the moment when information passes from one human to another. And despite mountains of data, the safest handovers are still those where people speak, ask clarifying questions, and check mutual understanding. At Salford Royal, Fiona conducted her midday handover by naming both clinical priorities and emotional cues: "Bed three is stable but frightened"; "Bed eight is clinically improved but angry about the delay." The decision-support system could not record these subtleties. Yet they were essential for the next shift's success. Relationship work expanded the dataset in ways no model could do.

Scripts for difficult conversations function similarly. Their purpose is to create structure around discomfort without removing humanity. Consider the simple opener used by some NHS teams: "I may be wrong, but I'm worried about…" This phrasing lowers defensiveness by embedding humility. Or the stakeholder-alignment question used in tense meetings: "What outcome would feel fair to all of us, even if imperfect?" These are not tricks. They are tools that create the conditions for trust by acknowledging the relational dimension of work. They also reflect a fundamental truth: good conversations reduce system-level risk. They prevent misunderstandings from escalating into operational failures.

Research supports this. A 2017 study by the Health Foundation on multidisciplinary care teams in England found that communication quality strongly correlated with patient outcomes. The visible behaviours included proactive clarification, explicit turn-taking, and respectful pushback when concerns arose. Automation did not diminish these behaviours. It made them more critical. As systems grow more complex, the relational load increases. More coordination is required, not less.

A second example, from outside healthcare, reinforces the point. In 2018, Airbus teams in Toulouse adopted a decision-support platform for component integration on the A350 line. The platform surfaced sequencing conflicts earlier than before. But engineers reported that the biggest gains came not from the tool itself but from the way it changed conversations. Daily stand-ups shifted from status updates to mutual commitments: "If I alter this component by 3 p.m., can you adapt your fixture tomorrow morning?" The system highlighted issues; the relationships resolved them. Machines accelerated detection. Humans negotiated action.

Yet relationship work is fragile. It can be misapplied or overestimated. A limitation appears when teams mistake harmony for alignment. Overly polite groups avoid difficult conversations, preserving surface-level trust while undermining real progress. A 2021 retrospective at a major UK charity revealed that its digital transformation programme faltered not because of poor technical decisions but because stakeholders hesitated to voice concerns about unrealistic timelines. Relationship work requires candour, not comfort. To reconcile this, mature teams adopt scripts that institutionalise respectful challenge: "Can you walk me through your confidence on that point?" or "What assumption here feels most exposed?" These phrases introduce friction without hostility. They turn dissent into inquiry.

The motif of the handover returns. Every complex handover blends data with narrative. It demands that people align on what information means, not just what it is. Machines excel at transmitting the "what". They cannot concord on the "why". And without concord on the "why", systems drift. Trust fractures. Decisions slow.

As this subchapter comes to its close, imagine Fiona at Salford Royal repeating her final handover of the day. The system displays a neat list of tasks, scores, and alerts. She adds the human layer: "Mr Ahmed trusts you; he asked for you by name"; "Mrs Clarke is grieving; go slow with her tonight." These remarks carry no numerical weight, yet they shape the night shift's success. They matter.

One unresolved question lingers, quiet but decisive: when algorithms coordinate the tasks, who will coordinate the people—and how will they know what to say when it matters most?

Learning as a daily loop

How can someone attend forty hours of formal training and still be outperformed by a colleague who spends ninety minutes a week in deliberate practice? The paradox is uncomfortable because it challenges a cherished belief: that reskilling is something we do in big, respectable chunks—courses, certificates, programmes—that can be ticked off and filed away. Yet when you look closely at who actually adapts fastest to new tools and environments, a different pattern emerges. They do not learn once. They loop.

Picture a sales representative in Leeds in early 2023, working for a mid-sized software firm selling compliance tools to financial services. Her company has just rolled out a generative AI assistant, complete with a "prompt library" of suggested questions for drafting outreach emails, summarising meetings, and tailoring proposals. Most of her colleagues try it once, smile at the novelty, and then revert to their old templates. She does something else. Every Friday morning from 8:30 to 10:00, she blocks out her calendar for a simple routine: scan three examples of effective prompts, practise adapting them to one real prospect, ship one email or proposal generated with the tool, and reflect briefly on the response data from the previous week. Three months later, her reply rates have doubled, and her average deal cycle has shortened by nearly a week. Her job title has not changed. Her tools are the same as everyone else's. The difference lies in the loop she runs.

The automation age makes this loop more than a productivity trick. When tools evolve quickly, skills decay faster. Knowledge about a model's capabilities becomes outdated within a quarter. New features appear without ceremony. The only sustainable response is to treat reskilling as a habit, not an event—a rhythm woven into the fabric of work. The motif that will thread through this section is simple: the small weekly laboratory. Not a glamorous lab with white coats and complex instruments, but a modest recurring space where you test, adjust, and internalise.

Historically, the organisations that have adapted best to technological change have done exactly this, often without using the language of "loops". Toyota's production system in Toyota City, formalised from the 1950s onwards, is frequently described as a set of principles—Just-in-Time, Jidoka, Kanban—but at its heart lies a disciplined learning rhythm. Front-line workers use "andon" cords to stop the line when they detect a problem, then participate in brief "hansei" reflection meetings to identify root causes. Show, name, explain, implication. Show: a worker pulls the andon cord when a part is misaligned. Name: the team gathers for a quick problem-solving session. Explain: they do not wait for an annual review or a training seminar; they adjust the process immediately, often within minutes or hours. Implication: quality improves because learning happens in small, continuous loops embedded in daily work, not in occasional training events detached from practice.

Contrast this with the way many knowledge workers approach reskilling. A bank in London commissions a three-day course on data storytelling in May, complete with polished slide decks and certificates. Attendance is high. Engagement looks good. Six months later, very few analysts actually present differently. Slide decks still overflow with crowded charts. Narratives remain thin. What happened? The event felt like learning, but no loop followed. There was scanning (new frameworks), but no sustained practising with feedback, no shipping of new styles into real meetings, no structured reflection on whether executives made better decisions as a result. Without the loop, the forgetting curve described by psychologist Hermann Ebbinghaus in 1885 does its quiet work. Most of the material evaporates within days.

The 90-minute weekly cycle proposed here—scan, practise, ship, reflect—is designed to counter that evaporation and harness compounding effects. Scan is about exposure: deliberately encountering a small number of new patterns, prompts, or techniques rather than passively consuming endless tips. Practise means applying one of those patterns to a live problem, not a hypothetical case. Ship means sending the result into the world where it can succeed or fail in contact with reality. Reflect means comparing intention with outcome, asking "What did I expect?" and "What actually happened?" The behaviours are concrete: blocking time in the calendar, opening a log of experiments, tracking a single metric like response rate or error count.

The sales representative in Leeds turned her Friday slot into a miniature laboratory. One week she tested prompts that personalised outreach using specific regulatory changes; the following week she experimented with prompts that prioritised narrative over detail. She did not treat the AI as a magic box. She treated it as a partner in a controlled trial. After six cycles, she noticed that emails opening with a short, scenario-based story about audit risk generated more replies than those listing features, regardless of the technical sophistication of the prompt. Her learning was not "AI is powerful." Her learning was, "For this segment, story-driven openings outperform bullet-point lists by about 30 per cent." That is a sharper, more actionable form of knowledge, and it arrived through repetition.

Two named examples from outside sales show how this pattern scales. In 2003, Google formalised its "20 per cent time" policy at its Mountain View headquarters, allowing engineers to spend a day a week on projects outside their core responsibilities. The practice has since been mythologised, but its most important feature was not the percentage. It was the regularity. Engineers created loops in which they scanned new ideas, practised small prototypes, shipped them internally, and reflected on which gained traction. Products such as Gmail, first released in April 2004, and AdSense grew from these loops. The company did not run a single "innovation course" and then hope for the best. It built a weekly structure that treated learning as part of the job.

A second example comes from healthcare. From 2010 onwards, several NHS trusts, including Northumbria Healthcare NHS Foundation Trust, adopted regular "Schwartz Rounds" named after the Schwartz Center for Compassionate Healthcare in Boston. These are monthly, structured forums where clinical and non-clinical staff discuss the emotional and social dimensions of care. At first glance, they might seem unrelated to reskilling. Yet they model the same loop: scan (hearing stories from different roles), practise (trying new communication approaches on the ward), ship (bringing those approaches into daily care), reflect (returning to the rounds to discuss what changed). Studies reported improvements in staff empathy and reductions in burnout (Maben et al., 2018). Again, the pattern holds: small, regular cycles beat occasional interventions.

There is, however, a credible counter-example. Many organisations run agile rituals—weekly sprints, retrospectives, stand-ups—that should function as learning loops but degenerate into rote status updates. A software firm in Dublin, for instance, introduced retrospectives at the end of each two-week sprint with the intention of driving continuous improvement. Within a year, the meetings had become rushed, with generic comments like "communication could be better" and little follow-through. The loop existed in form but not in substance. People went through the motions without committing to concrete experiments in the next cycle. Learning stalled.

Reconciling this limitation requires attention to two elements: specificity and stakes. Specificity means naming one change per cycle, not ten; stakes mean tying that change to a visible metric. The Leeds sales representative did not attempt to overhaul her entire approach each week. She tested one prompt pattern and measured one outcome. The Toyota worker investigated one root cause at a time. The NHS team in Northumbria tried one conversational shift. When loops stay small and tied to visible results, they remain alive. When they expand into vague aspiration, they die.

The motif of the small laboratory returns. A laboratory is not a place where everything succeeds; it is a place where failure is expected and informative. The same applies to personal reskilling. In March, the sales representative tested a prompt that heavily referenced technical jargon. Her reply rate dropped. Rather than abandoning the tool or blaming the market, she treated the result as data. In her next cycle, she simplified language and anchored messages in practical outcomes. The metric recovered. Over time, these micro-adjustments produced a body of tacit knowledge: an internal map of what worked for which clients, supported by her own experiments rather than generic advice.

The psychological dimension matters too. Event-based reskilling often creates spikes of anxiety. A three-day course implies that everyone should emerge transformed; when they do not, they quietly label themselves "not technical", "not creative", or "bad with data". Loops make improvement mundane. Ninety minutes a week is too small to feel heroic, yet large enough to accumulate. This lowers the emotional barrier to starting. You do not have to reinvent yourself; you only have to run the next experiment.

Learning loops also interact with organisational power. People who run them consistently become more resilient to structural shocks. When a new automation tool arrives, they already have a slot in which to explore it. When a process changes, they already maintain a log of experiments and observations. Their value is less tied to a specific technology and more to their capacity to absorb new ones. That capacity becomes a kind of invisible capital.

Yet there is an unresolved tension. Loops require protected time, and most workplaces are not designed to protect anything that does not show immediate output. The 90-minute slot is constantly at risk—from urgent emails, from meetings scheduled over it, from the individual's own guilt about not being "available". Here, leadership design matters. When managers treat looping as legitimate work rather than indulgence, they shift the norm. At Google, 20 per cent time survived because leaders used it themselves and celebrated outcomes. At Toyota, problem-solving sessions are treated as integral, not optional. At Northumbria, Schwartz Rounds occupy real clinical time.

As automation spreads, the value of these small laboratories only increases. Tools will continue to change. Interfaces will continue to mutate. Models will continue to surprise. The question is not whether professionals can accumulate enough knowledge once to stay safe. They cannot. The question is whether they can build a rhythm in which learning, testing, and adjusting become as ordinary as checking email.

So the sales representative in Leeds opens her calendar for the coming quarter. The Friday slot is there, recurring. She renames it "Lab". She guards it from meetings. She adds a short note at the top of her experiment log: *Scan, practise, ship, reflect.* The loop waits.

One question hangs over her schedule, and over yours: when the week fills with noise, what will guarantee that your small laboratory survives—and with it, your capacity to keep pace with the systems evolving around you?

Chapter 3
Redesigning Your Workflow

On a wet Tuesday morning in Bristol, a solicitor named Hannah Carter sat at her desk surrounded by the usual mountain of disclosure material: scanned contracts, witness emails, financial schedules, and the assorted detritus of a commercial dispute that had ballooned far beyond proportion. Her predecessors would have spent days combing through each document by hand, eyes blurring as they hunted for contradictions or buried admissions. Hannah, by contrast, opened a slim AI interface trained on the firm's precedents. She fed the model the first tranche of files, instructed it to flag time-sensitive anomalies, and watched the results populate her screen. Nothing final, nothing binding—just a triage layer. The drudgery shrank. The shape of her day shifted. She still read the most delicate documents personally. She still took responsibility for judgement. But she reclaimed hours she had previously surrendered to administrative grind, and she did so without loosening her grip on risk. It was the smallest of revolutions, visible only to her. Yet this quiet moment captures the chapter's thesis: workflows do not change themselves. We redesign them.

The shift feels subtle until you stand inside it. Across industries—from radiology suites in Birmingham to HR departments in Edinburgh—professionals are discovering that the boundary between their labour and their tools is no longer fixed. It can be redrawn. Tasks that once belonged exclusively to humans now sit partly with machines, partly with checklists, partly with structured prompts. What remains fully human are the choices: where to place the line, where to tighten oversight, where to surrender friction, where to retain it. Work becomes a system of flows rather than a stack of responsibilities. And the people who thrive are those who learn to map, question, and re-engineer that system with precision.

This chapter enters that terrain by asking a deceptively simple question: if you could rebuild your workflow from scratch—step by step, decision by decision—how would you design it? The question matters because modern work has grown thick with inherited habits, many of them relics of a pre-automation age. Meetings that survived long after their purpose decayed. Reviews that expanded without improving quality. Forms and approvals created in moments of crisis and never retired. Automation tempts us to graft new tools onto old patterns. But grafts rarely hold. Real transformation begins further upstream, with task mapping: the careful disassembly of work into what you sense, what you synthesise, what you decide, what you act upon, and what you learn from afterwards. Only once you see these steps clearly can you ask which ones you should assist, which you should automate, and which you must continue to own.

Consider the radiologist in Manchester using AI for second reads. The machine scans thousands of pixels per second and highlights possible lesions. The radiologist reviews the suggestions, discards false positives, and interprets patterns through clinical experience. The machine reduces oversight fatigue; the human corrects automated overconfidence. The arrangement may look simple, but it rests on a profound principle: humans stay in the loop where stakes, ambiguity, or values are high. The radiologist does not abdicate responsibility. She redistributes attention. Her workflow becomes safer not because the machine is flawless, but because the partnership is designed with guardrails, handoffs, and clear boundaries of accountability.

This principle scales far beyond medicine. A recruiter in Dublin builds a reusable prompt pack that screens CVs for role fit, extracts structured summaries, and drafts initial interview questions. The prompts are written like briefs—role context, goals, guardrails, examples, tests. The machine accelerates comparison; the recruiter preserves fairness. Instead of drowning in repetitive screening, she spends her time evaluating nuance: tone, motivation, trajectory. The tool handles volume. She handles meaning. Her workflow becomes more humane precisely because she gave part of it to a system that neither judges nor tires.

And yet, as workflows change, something else becomes unavoidable: evidence. When machines help produce an outcome, the question of *how* they helped becomes a matter of record, not opinion. In regulated environments—from finance to healthcare to government—quality and audit trails shift from administrative chores to structural safeguards. A compliance team in London learns this quickly when it adopts lightweight logs documenting which models were used, which versions, and what instructions guided them. The logs take minutes to maintain but transform the team's relationship with auditors. Transparency replaces suspicion. Speed no longer conflicts with accountability. The workflow becomes traceable, not bureaucratic.

What links these examples—Hannah's triage, the radiologist's second read, the recruiter's prompt pack, the compliance team's logs—is the recognition that workflows are no longer neutral. They are strategic. The choice to automate a single micro-task can shift error rates, morale, time allocation, and even ethical exposure. The choice to keep a human present can protect dignity, mitigate bias, and preserve trust. The choice to document an interaction can determine whether a process withstands scrutiny when something goes wrong. Every workflow is a philosophy in motion.

The middle sections of this chapter will walk through the architecture of such redesign: how to break your work into its atomic units; how to examine each unit for opportunities and risks; how to embed "human-in-the-loop" patterns that reflect not just operational logic but moral clarity; how to treat prompts as living design documents; how to construct audit trails that protect both speed and integrity. The aim is not to overwhelm the reader with tools but to offer a vocabulary—clean, pragmatic, durable—for thinking about work as a set of flows you can orchestrate, not merely absorb.

A quiet motif runs through everything that follows: the handoff. In modern systems, success does not depend only on the intelligence of each step but on the quality of the transitions between them. Between machine and human. Between one human and another. Between decision and action. Between action and learning. Poorly designed handoffs cause friction, confusion, and blame. Well-designed handoffs create coherence. They allow individuals to operate at the top of their capability without carrying unnecessary cognitive load. They distribute attention instead of scattering it. They stabilise complexity.

As the chapter draws toward its final movement, the focus shifts from method to mindset. The shift required here is not technical but conceptual: a willingness to see your workflow not as a fixed identity but as a living organism, one that can—and should—be shaped deliberately. It requires the humility to question your own habits and the confidence to reconfigure them. It requires understanding that automation does not diminish the human but repositions the human at the points where discernment, care, and judgement matter most.

And so a question hovers as we step into the details: if your workflow is the skeleton of your working life—its routines, its decisions, its rhythms—what might be possible if you rebuilt that skeleton with intention instead of inheritance?

Task mapping

In January 2022, at the London offices of Clyde & Co, a commercial solicitor named Hannah Patel faced a discovery deadline that would once have consumed her entire week. The case involved more than 42,000 documents—contracts, internal messages, spreadsheets, and board correspondence—dumped into a shared drive with the usual warning: *review everything*. Previously, this meant late nights and mechanical reading, hoping that nothing critical slipped past tired eyes. This time, Hannah did something different. She opened a machine-learning review tool, instructed it to surface anomalies, cluster duplicates, and highlight communications around key dates, and watched as the first structured results appeared within minutes. But she did not surrender judgement. She designed a workflow: the system would *sense* the corpus; she would *synthesise* its signals; the system would *assist* the first pass; she would *own* the final review. The drudgery fell away. The risk stayed where it belonged—with her. Task mapping had quietly rewritten the shape of her labour.

Scenes like this are becoming common, yet the underlying logic is often misunderstood. Automation is not a monolith sweeping across work; it is a set of component capabilities that slot into the stages of a task. When people feel overwhelmed by tools, it is usually because they have not broken their work down far enough. Complexity lives in lumps. Clarity lives in sequences. Task mapping forces the sequence into view.

Begin with the structure itself: sense, synthesise, decide, act, learn. It is not novel. Engineers at Bletchley Park in 1943 used a version of it to break ciphers—first acquiring raw signals, then grouping patterns, then deciding which machine settings to test, then running the test, then analysing errors. What *is* new is the ease with which machines now operate within each stage. Show, name, explain, implication. Show: a model scans thousands of documents in seconds. Name: it performs sensing. Explain: sensing is the stage where volume overwhelms humans. Implication: giving that stage to a model frees human attention for what follows—synthesis and judgement.

Hannah's workday is a practical example. The model sensed: identifying clusters, timestamps, and unusual phrasing. Hannah synthesised: reading across clusters, noting inconsistencies, linking emails to contracts. The model assisted decision-making by flagging anomalies. Hannah owned the final decisions: which documents were relevant, which claims stood, which lines of argument could survive scrutiny. She acted by preparing the case strategy. And at the end of the cycle, she ran a short review of which prompts and filters had performed well, adjusting her setup for the next round. Each stage was visible. Each stage had a designated owner. Each stage had a clear handoff.

This clarity is rarer than it sounds. Many professionals carry out their tasks as undifferentiated blobs of work. The consequence is predictable: people either automate too much—handing ambiguous decisions to tools that cannot tolerate ambiguity—or too little, drowning in work that machines could handle safely. Task mapping prevents these extremes by making every stage explicit.

Two further examples show the power of this structure. In April 2019, radiologists at the Royal Free Hospital in London piloted an AI system that highlighted potential pulmonary nodules on CT scans. The system did the sensing: scanning images, detecting shapes, flagging suspicious regions. The radiologist did the synthesis: integrating those flags with clinical history. The model made no decisions. It merely suggested where attention might go. The radiologist acted by confirming or dismissing the flags. After each shift, the team reviewed false positives and false negatives, adjusting thresholds and calibrating expectations. That final stage—the quiet act of learning—proved decisive. Error rates dropped because the workflow had a memory. Hospitals that treated the model as a black box did not see the same improvements.

A second example comes from outside healthcare. In July 2021, analysts at the Bank of England investigated patterns in mortgage-risk data using a classification model. The model sensed—sorting millions of rows. Analysts synthesised by comparing anomalous clusters with macroeconomic indicators. Decisions were owned by humans because risk classification carries regulatory and ethical stakes. After acting—publishing a technical report—they examined where the model's outputs diverged from historical patterns and updated their guidelines. Here the visible behaviours included version tracking, annotated notebooks, and structured after-action reviews. These behaviours are the practical expression of the learn stage. Without them, the exercise would have produced insight once and then faded.

The counter-example is equally instructive. A major retailer in 2020 attempted to automate customer-support routing. They handed sensing, synthesis, and decision-making to a single system. Emails were classified incorrectly. High-risk complaints were deprioritised. Customers received irrelevant responses. Staff intervened only at the act stage, far too late. The workflow collapsed because the mapping was absent. They automated the wrong stages. Reconcile this failure by noting that automation succeeds not when it does the most work, but when it does the right work.

A quiet motif threads through these stories: the line. Every workflow has a line between what the machine should do and what you must never surrender. The line is not static. It moves with context. In high-stakes environments—legal, medical, safety-critical—humans always own the decide stage. In high-volume environments—marketing, support, logistics—machines may own large parts of sensing and initial synthesis. The discipline lies in drawing the line consciously. The risk lies in letting it drift.

Task mapping also gives you a vocabulary for marking each stage: assist, automate, or own. Assist means the machine offers suggestions you can accept or reject. Automate means the machine performs the task reliably without oversight.

Own means the task rests with you because consequences travel through judgement, ethics, or interpretation. These distinctions matter. They shape accountability. They shape error tolerance. They shape how you spend your attention.

Hannah marked sensing as automate. She marked synthesis as assist: the model clustered and summarised, but she integrated. She marked decision-making as own. And she marked learning as own-with-assist: the system tracked which prompts produced high-quality flags, but she interpreted what the next cycle should change. This structure gave her control without forcing her to do work that added no value. It also protected her from a common trap: the illusion of oversight. When humans attempt to "review" thousands of automated suggestions without a clear mapping, they often rubber-stamp. Task mapping prevents this by reducing volume before human review begins.

The benefits grow over time. Workflows with clear mapping reveal waste—duplicate checks, unnecessary approvals, tasks that linger through inertia. They also reveal seams where subtle improvements compound. For instance, small tweaks to the synthesis stage can reduce error in the decide stage disproportionately. Likewise, adding a 10-minute learn stage to the weekly cycle can save hours in sensing the following week. Task mapping is not only a diagnostic tool; it is a lever.

There is a philosophical depth to this approach. It asks you to see your work as a system of transformations, not a series of chores. You receive inputs. You transform them through thought. You act. You learn. Each transformation carries opportunity. Each handoff carries risk. In complex environments, the shape of these transformations matters more than the tools themselves. A poorly designed workflow filled with excellent tools still fails.

The motif of the line returns here. When you draw the line consciously, you reclaim authorship of your own workflow. You move from reacting to your tools to orchestrating them. You decide how much cognitive weight to give to machines. You decide where to inject your judgement. You decide how to embed evidence and reflection. The line becomes not a barrier but a design element.

As we approach the closing movement, the solicitor in London reappears. Her discovery triage is complete, but she pauses before closing the file. She updates her notes: which clusters required the most correction, which anomaly prompts produced noise, which time windows were most fruitful. She adjusts her mapping for the next case. The system did not teach her this. The mapping did.

A question lingers, sharp and necessary: when your work spans dozens of tasks and tools, where will you draw the line—and what will change if you redraw it tomorrow?

Human-in-the-loop

At 7:42 a.m. on 12 March 2021, at Addenbrooke's Hospital in Cambridge, consultant radiologist Dr Rebecca Harrington opened a chest CT scan flagged overnight by an

AI triage system. The software—deployed across the Trust that January—had labelled the image "high priority" with a confidence score of 0.87, highlighting a faint, irregular opacity in the upper lobe. The mark was subtle; under ordinary workloads it might have waited hours for review. Harrington enlarged the slice, traced the contour with her stylus, and compared it with the previous scan. The AI was right about the region of interest but wrong about its origin. Not a malignant nodule. Post-inflammatory scarring. She downgraded the alert and dictated a note for the supervising oncologist. Two minutes saved, one false alarm corrected, and a quiet confirmation of a broader principle: where stakes, ambiguity, or values are high, machines can narrow the field of attention, but humans must remain in the loop.

The Cambridge case is modest, but its significance is not. It shows the essential choreography of modern decision-making: the system senses, the human interprets; the system highlights, the human confirms; the system accelerates, the human calibrates risk. Harrington did not rubber-stamp the alert; she interrogated it. She did not distrust the model reflexively; she used it to direct her scrutiny. Her expertise shaped the final judgement. The collaboration worked not because the model was powerful, but because the workflow preserved a boundary—soft where speed mattered, firm where consequences did.

This boundary becomes the motif of this chapter: the gate. Every complex workflow has one. In medicine, the gate stands at diagnosis. In aviation, at take-off clearance. In finance, at risk classification. In law, at final argument. The gate marks the moment where responsibility snaps into focus. Machines may advise, summarise, or pre-screen, but only humans can carry responsibility for what happens next. Gate work requires contextual knowledge, professional norms, and moral agency. Lose sight of the gate, and you lose control of the system.

To understand why the human-in-the-loop pattern matters, show, name, explain, implication. Show: a radiologist reviews an AI-highlighted region. Name: she performs gatekeeping. Explain: gatekeeping ensures that automated detections are interpreted through domain knowledge, not merely through statistical association. Implication: human judgement prevents systematic bias from sliding unnoticed into high-stakes outcomes.

Extend this principle through a second example. In 2018, the University of Pittsburgh Medical Center integrated an early-warning algorithm into its electronic health record system. The model predicted risk of sepsis up to six hours before clinical deterioration. Nurses saw alerts on handheld devices. Yet the system succeeded only because the clinical team inserted a human gate: nurses validated each alert in conversation with physicians, documenting whether the model's trigger matched the patient's presentation. The behaviour was deliberate: they refused to escalate patients on algorithmic authority alone. Over the first year, false positives fell, unnecessary antibiotic use decreased, and nurses reported higher confidence in triage decisions. The algorithm did not replace clinical judgement; it sharpened and accelerated it.

Contrast this with a counter-example. In 2020, a major US insurer briefly piloted an automated claims assessment tool that recommended denial for cases deemed "low likelihood of complication". Claims officers, overwhelmed by volume, often accepted the tool's recommendation without investigating borderline cases. The result: a spike in appeals and a public backlash after journalists uncovered denials that ignored crucial contextual information. The system had removed the human gate at the wrong moment—where ambiguity and ethical stakes demanded scrutiny. Without a human-in-the-loop, efficiency overwhelmed fairness. Reconciliation lies here: automation improves outcomes when it narrows uncertainty, not when it outruns responsibility.

The handoff between human and machine is where risk concentrates. Poor handoffs create blind spots; good ones distribute vigilance. Harrington at Addenbrooke's followed a structured handoff discipline: she noted whether the AI's highlight was accepted, rejected, or flagged for review; she annotated why; she copied the decision into the system's feedback log. That visible behaviour is the foundation of confidence calibration. Over time, radiologists learn when to trust the system's strengths—detecting faint or irregular patterns—and when to override it. The model, in turn, improves from the feedback. The loop tightens. Confidence grows because accountability is shared but not diluted.

Human-in-the-loop workflows rely on guardrails that are as cultural as they are technical. One guardrail is scope. The model must have a defined operational envelope: the situations it handles well, the situations where it must hand back control, and the situations where it must remain silent. A second guardrail is escalation: when the model encounters uncertainty beyond thresholds, the workflow must shift decisively to human judgement. A third guardrail is transparency: the system must show enough of its reasoning—through exemplars, confidence scores, or saliency maps—to allow the human to interrogate it meaningfully.

These guardrails exist well beyond medicine. In 2022, at the Competition and Markets Authority in London, analysts piloted a natural-language processing tool to screen merger documents. The system extracted entities, highlighted potential conflicts, and clustered themes. But the analysts implemented a strict gate at the synthesis stage. No automated summary could enter a case report unless an analyst manually reviewed its supporting snippets. They used a handoff checklist—"Have I seen the underlying text? What assumptions did the model make? Which interpretations remain ambiguous?"—to prevent automated misreadings from entering regulatory decisions. Speed increased, but so did scrutiny.

A related example comes from journalism. At the Associated Press, where automated earnings reports have been produced since 2014, editors review each generated draft. They check not just accuracy but angle—whether the text frames company performance fairly, avoids unintended inferences, and aligns with editorial guidelines. The model accelerates data extraction; editors retain control of meaning. Here gatekeeping protects public trust.

But human-in-the-loop workflows have limitations. Humans can become complacent, assuming that a system's "high-confidence" label is synonymous with correctness. In a 2016 study at MIT, researchers Comber and Greenleaf found that analysts reviewing AI-assisted satellite imagery became *less* accurate when the model's confidence was displayed. They over-relied on the score and missed obvious anomalies. To reconcile this risk, systems can suppress confidence labels for ambiguous cases or introduce "challenge" tasks that require analysts to justify acceptance. The guardrail becomes psychological as much as procedural: do not let confidence override diligence.

The quiet motif of the gate returns. Gates require rituals. In aviation, pilots follow call-and-response checklists before critical transitions. In medicine, surgeons conduct "time-outs" before incisions. In software operations, senior engineers review severity escalations before paging teams. These rituals are not bureaucratic performance. They are the behavioural scaffolding that keeps humans attentive when stakes rise. Human-in-the-loop workflows need equivalent rituals: deliberate pauses, structured queries, and explicit acknowledgements of responsibility.

Consider the radiologist again. After reviewing the CT scan, Harrington did not simply close the case. She documented her reasoning, sent a short message to the multidisciplinary team, and entered feedback into the AI system's audit log. This small act—the written articulation of judgement—is itself a ritual. It reinforces the boundary between suggestion and decision. It preserves a trail for future review. It teaches the system and the team.

Now shift the setting. In November 2022, a logistics company in Rotterdam implemented an optimisation system to allocate warehouse tasks. The model made efficient assignments but sometimes produced sequences that were physically impractical—heavy items stacked above fragile goods, or tasks clustered far from rest areas. Supervisors intervened. They used a "handoff board" where staff could annotate why a model-generated schedule was rejected: heat fatigue, aisle blockages, forklift availability. Within months, the model improved. But the deeper success was cultural: workers saw themselves not as executors but as co-designers. The human-in-the-loop was not a concession. It was a commitment.

Human-in-the-loop workflows also reshape accountability. When systems become part of decision-making, organisations must clarify who is responsible for what. A clinician signs off diagnoses. A regulator signs off reports. A recruiter signs off hiring decisions. Machines support, but humans remain accountable. This asymmetry is not a flaw. It reflects the moral structure of work. Responsibility cannot be automated.

As we approach the closing movement, the motif of the gate sharpens. Every workflow must decide where its gate sits. Some gates should be close to the data—triage, filtering, monitoring. Others belong near consequences—diagnosis, sentencing, approval. Draw the gate wrong, and the system drifts. Draw it well, and machine intelligence becomes an ally rather than a liability.

And so a question hovers, quiet yet decisive, over every profession beginning to integrate automated tools: when the model presents its best guess with impeccable speed, what will stop you, steady your attention, and remind you that the final decision still carries your name?

Prompt craft as process

At 09:15 on 17 February 2023, in the Manchester offices of a midsized recruitment firm, senior talent partner Olivia Mercer opened her laptop to find another queue of sixty-seven CVs submitted overnight. Her brief was a familiar one: produce a shortlist for a hard-to-fill data analyst role by the end of the day. For years she had relied on meticulous manual review, colour-coded spreadsheets, and a quick calibration call with the hiring manager. But the volume had swollen. The stakes had risen. And the firm could no longer justify slow cycles. That morning, instead of working line by line, Olivia deployed a prompt pack she had refined over several months—structured instructions governing how her AI assistant should extract competencies, flag ambiguities, and generate consistent, fair interview questions. The system followed her design: it processed the CVs using her brief, highlighted discrepancies, and produced standardised candidate summaries. Olivia read the outputs closely, tested edge cases, and adjusted two guardrails. By lunchtime, she had a defensible shortlist. No corners were cut. No judgement was surrendered. The prompt pack was not a script. It was a process—one she shaped deliberately.

The Manchester case is emblematic of a broader shift. As language models became widely accessible after November 2022—when OpenAI released ChatGPT in San Francisco—professionals discovered that the quality of an AI's output hinges less on its raw capacity and more on the structure of the instructions guiding it. A prompt is not merely a question; it is a brief. And a brief is a design artefact. Clear briefs yield clarity. Vague briefs yield chaos. We see this principle everywhere in creative and analytical work, yet many users approach AI systems as though they were oracles rather than collaborators. They feed half-formed requests into a model and are surprised when the results mirror their ambiguity.

Prompt craft forces a reckoning with intent. It demands precision. And, crucially, it treats prompts not as one-off commands but as components of a workflow that can be versioned, tested, and improved.

Consider the structure Olivia used: role, goal, guardrails, examples, tests. Show, name, explain, implication. Show: she instructed the AI to behave as a neutral assessor trained on the firm's competency framework. Name: that is the *role*. Explain: she gave the model a perspective, shaping tone and priorities. Implication: clarity of role reduces drift, ensuring that outputs align with professional standards rather than generic clichés.

Goal came next. Olivia specified the outcome: extract evidence of analytical reasoning, communication clarity, and domain-relevant technical competence. The AI had an objective with boundaries. Without a goal, the system would have described candidates instead of evaluating them. Guardrails followed: no inference about age, nationality, or gaps without explicit evidence; flag unverifiable claims; summarise skills in standardised, comparable units. In sensitive domains like recruitment, guardrails are not optional. They are the ethical skeleton of the workflow.

Examples and tests closed the loop. Olivia provided two anonymised CV fragments—one strong, one borderline—with her own approved summaries. These functioned as exemplars. She then added "tests": stress prompts designed to expose failure modes, such as contradictory dates or inconsistent job titles. When outputs deviated from expectations, she iterated.

What is striking here is not the novelty. Editors have used style guides for decades. Programmers have used unit tests since at least the 1970s. The innovation lies in applying these disciplines to language interfaces—treating prompt craft as a process rather than an intuition.

The same logic appears in a different domain. In 2020, The Guardian in London published an editorial paragraph co-written with a language model. The editors gave the system a detailed brief: adopt a measured tone, avoid sensationalism, present arguments cautiously, and foreground human agency. The brief governed not just what the model produced but how the editors judged its adequacy. They refined phrasing, removed unintended assertions, and ensured fidelity to journalistic norms. The behaviour reveals the underlying truth: prompts are design constraints. Editors do not ask models to "write an article"; they sculpt instructions to elicit accountable, context-appropriate results.

But prompt craft does have limits. The temptation to over-specify is real. In 2022, researchers at Stanford University observed that hyper-detailed prompts often caused models to misinterpret priorities, producing cluttered, overqualified responses. Constraint became noise. The lesson is simple: prompts must focus attention, not overwhelm it. The craft lies in balancing direction with room for interpretation—much like writing a creative brief for a designer or commissioning a report from an analyst.

A quiet motif threads through these examples: the lens. A prompt is a lens shaping how a model "looks" at information. A clean lens sharpens. A dirty lens distorts.

Olivia's role specification, the Guardian's tone instructions, and the researchers' tests all demonstrate how prompts frame perception. When the lens is well designed, the model aligns with the human's conceptual frame. When the lens is sloppy, outputs degrade, fairness erodes, and trust dissolves.

Trust itself becomes visible through behaviours. Olivia inspected borderline cases personally. She cross-checked the model's extracted skills against the raw CVs. She compared summary lengths across candidates to ensure parity. These behaviours translate abstractions like "fairness" or "accountability" into practical decisions. Trust is not blind acceptance; it is verified consistency.

Prompt craft also restructures collaboration. When colleagues share prompt packs, they share reasoning patterns. In 2023, a design team at a London creative agency adopted shared prompt libraries for concept generation. The prompts included role specifications ("act as a typographic historian"), style constraints ("limit colour palettes to two complementary tones"), and evaluation tests ("contrast mood with brand narrative"). The pack created a unified starting point. Designers still curated final selections—they chose what carried story fit—but the collective lens reduced drift between team members, especially under deadline pressure.

The counter-example clarifies the stakes. In 2021, an American retailer used an unstructured prompt—"screen candidates for cultural fit"—to generate interview questions. The model returned vague, occasionally biased prompts because "cultural fit" itself is an incoherent instruction. Hiring managers misinterpreted the AI's output, assuming that the questions were neutral. Complaints followed. The problem was not the model. It was the prompt. The lens was so unclear that bias passed through unnoticed.

Reconciliation comes through rigour. Cultural fit is replaced by observable behaviours: collaboration under pressure, clarity of communication, conflict resolution. Once these are specified, the prompt becomes a brief, not a guess. This is the heart of the subchapter: prompt craft disciplines ambiguity. It forces the human to articulate what they value before they ask the machine to evaluate it.

The motif of the lens returns at the level of workflow. Prompts become assets—versioned, stored, auditable. Olivia maintained her prompt pack in a shared document. Each version was tagged with a date and a rationale for changes. She archived failure cases. She added "edge notes" describing common misinterpretations. She built, in effect, a living style guide for candidate assessment. By treating prompts as artefacts, not messages, she created institutional memory.

This mindset extends to other fields. In legal practice, lawyers build prompts to summarise precedents while complying with jurisdictional constraints. In research, analysts design prompts to test hypotheses by asking models to simulate counterfactuals under controlled assumptions. In government, policy teams construct prompts that require models to cite sources with dated references, reducing the risk of fabricated quotes. In each case, the artefact stabilises judgement.

But all artefacts need boundaries. Prompts cannot eliminate ambiguity. They can only shape it. Models trained on human data inherit its imperfections; even the most disciplined prompt cannot fully suppress unwanted associations. This is why the human remains in the loop. Olivia understands this. She reviews each shortlist personally. She calibrates the system's strengths—pattern extraction, summarisation—with her own strengths—context, nuance, long-term judgement.

As the piece moves toward its final movement, the motif sharpens: a prompt is a negotiation. It is an agreement between the human's intention and the machine's capacity. Every prompt asks: what do you want the system to attend to, and what do you insist on judging yourself?

Which brings us back to Olivia, closing her shortlist before presenting it to the hiring manager. She checks each candidate summary. She re-runs two tests. She refines a guardrail to prevent misclassification of hybrid roles. Then she saves her latest version of the prompt pack, marking the change: "v4.2—added ambiguity flag for overlapping skill clusters." The workflow evolves. The lens sharpens.

And so the question that lingers—quiet but insistent—is this: when you next ask a model to help you think, decide, or create, will your prompt be a message thrown into the void, or will it be a brief worthy of the decision it shapes?

Quality and audit trails

At 08:03 on 6 July 2022, in the Glasgow headquarters of Caledonian Mutual, senior compliance officer Laura McBride opened her audit dashboard to a familiar warning: thirty-two customer files required verification before the month-end regulatory review. Each file contained a mixture of human notes, AI-generated summaries, scanned evidence, and decision records. Two years earlier, this volume would have triggered an all-hands scramble. But that morning, the files were already tagged with lightweight logs—timestamps, model versions, prompt identifiers, human sign-offs. The compliance team had introduced the system in March 2022, after a difficult audit exposed gaps in documentation. The fix took less than a week to design. It now saved them dozens of hours per month, eliminated repeat queries from auditors, and, perhaps most importantly, restored confidence internally. Machines were helping the team, but the team could show how. The paper trail no longer lagged behind the workflow. It flowed with it.

The Glasgow case speaks to a deeper shift. As organisations integrate automated tools into critical decisions, the demand for transparent audit trails intensifies. Systems that once operated as black boxes can no longer hide their steps. Regulators, clients, and internal risk committees increasingly require evidence of lineage: *Which model shaped this recommendation? Which data did it rely on? Who reviewed it? Why was the final call made?* Where work becomes partially automated, accountability becomes partially procedural. And procedural accountability requires something deceptively simple: a record of what happened.

To understand why this matters, begin with a paradox. Models accelerate decisions, yet they can obscure the steps that produced those decisions. Humans, by contrast, decide more slowly but can explain their reasoning. When organisations combine the two, they risk getting neither speed nor transparency—unless they design explicit audit trails. The motif running through this subchapter is the ledger. A ledger captures lineage. A ledger clarifies responsibility. And in hybrid workflows, a ledger becomes the spine of institutional memory.

Consider versioning. Show: Caledonian Mutual tagged each model-generated summary with a model version number—v1.8, v1.9, v2.1—alongside the date and prompt pack used. Name: this practice is *version control*. Explain: version control distinguishes which system outputs belonged to which model behaviour. Implication: when an error surfaces, the team can trace it to a specific version rather than blaming the entire system.

Versioning is not merely a technical formality. In November 2020, the UK Home Office suspended an automated visa assessment tool after internal reviews found inconsistent decisions. A critical problem was the absence of historical version tracking. Without version lineage, the department could not document when classification behaviour changed or why. The lesson was hard-earned: systems that evolve must leave footprints. A model without a history has no accountability.

Data lineage is the next step in the ledger. It answers a simple question: *Which data shaped this output?* In 2019, the Financial Conduct Authority (FCA) in London began recommending that firms document the provenance of training data used in risk models, including source systems, update dates, and known limitations. The behaviour this guidance encourages is visible: analysts annotate datasets, list exclusion criteria, and note quality thresholds. The implication is significant. If a downstream decision is challenged, the organisation can demonstrate that it understood its inputs rather than treating them as neutral facts.

Contrast this with a counter-example. In 2021, a major e-commerce company faced scrutiny when its automated product-ranking system pushed counterfeit items above legitimate ones. The internal review discovered that the training data contained mislabelled products from a historical import log. Because lineage was undocumented, the team could not determine when the contamination entered the pipeline. The consequence was both operational and reputational. Reconciliation lies here: data lineage is not bureaucracy. It is defence.

Versioning and lineage anchor the ledger, but sign-offs animate it. Sign-offs mark responsibility. They show who read what, who approved what, and who understood the implications. In the Glasgow compliance team, each AI-generated summary required a human signature before entering the permanent record. The behaviour was simple: a brief annotation—accepted, modified, or rejected—with a sentence explaining the decision. The annotation took less than thirty seconds. Yet it transformed the audit conversation. Instead of confronting a tangle of automated outputs, auditors encountered a clear chain of reasoning.

Two further examples illustrate the breadth of this practice. In 2018, the Royal Free London NHS Foundation Trust documented human oversight steps in its deployment of a clinical decision-support tool. Each model recommendation was paired with a clinician's comment, linking the system's suggestion to the final diagnosis. The behaviour allowed the Trust to demonstrate that clinicians remained accountable. In 2020, the European Central Bank introduced a requirement for "model owner attestations" in supervisory reporting workflows, compelling teams to sign off annually on model behaviour, assumptions, and limitations. These attestations formalised what had previously been tacit. They turned professional judgement into a traceable artefact.

The counter-example clarifies the stakes. In 2022, an American mortgage lender abandoned its automated underwriting pilot after auditors flagged "unexplained variance" in loan approvals. The issue was not bias in the model. It was the absence of sign-off logs. Analysts had validated outputs manually, but they kept their notes in private documents, not in the system. When auditors asked for justification, no structured record existed. The lesson is structural: undocumented scrutiny might as well not exist.

Returning to the ledger motif, the key insight is that audit trails need not be heavy. Lightweight logs, like those adopted in Glasgow, often outperform complex systems because they integrate with real workflows instead of sitting adjacent to them. The logs captured five things: the source file; the model or tool used; the prompt or parameter set; the human correction; the final sign-off. That was enough. The behaviour was habitual, not burdensome. And because the logs were versioned, the compliance team could reconstruct decision lineage months later.

Audit trails also shape organisational psychology. When records are clear, accountability feels shared, not punitive. People document their reasoning because the system expects it, not because they fear review. This mindset is crucial in high-stakes environments where over-automation can fade the human presence. A ledger restores that presence by inviting explicit thought. Each log becomes a moment of reflection: Did the model assist, or did it mislead? Did I rely too much on its summary? Should this decision have triggered escalation?

Yet the ledger has boundaries. Too much detail becomes noise. Too many mandatory fields slow work. A system that asks the human to annotate everything ends up with annotations that mean nothing. The balance lies in identifying the minimal record that captures the essential lineage. Caledonian Mutual learned this during its first attempt: an early prototype included twelve fields. Staff ignored half. The team refined the log to five. Completion rose to 98 per cent within two weeks. A clean ledger protects quality. A bloated ledger undermines it.

At the end of this subchapter, the motif sharpens into a question about traceability. As automated systems proliferate—summarising, classifying, advising—how will organisations show the path from input to decision? How will they reconstruct the steps when something goes wrong? How will they assure clients, regulators, and themselves that decisions are not drifting beyond oversight?

And so a final question remains—not abstract, but immediate: in your own workflow, if someone asked tomorrow how a machine helped shape your decision, could you show them the ledger?

Chapter 4
Thriving in the AI-Driven Economy

On a Thursday evening in late September, in a quiet flat in Norwich, a secondary-school English teacher named Carla Howard watched the blue progress bar inch across her laptop screen. She had just uploaded the draft of a short online course—*How to Read Fiction Like a Writer*—that she'd built during the late hours of her summer holiday. She did not intend to resign from the classroom. She wasn't chasing viral fame. What she wanted was optionality: a second income stream that respected her craft, absorbed the elastic hours of term time, and gave her room to grow without uprooting the life she valued. With a simple set of AI tools, she had storyboarded the modules, sharpened the learning outcomes, refined her examples, and stress-tested her assignments. The core ideas were hers; the polish and scaffolding were accelerated. When the course went live, she earned her first £180 within three days. It wasn't the money that mattered. It was the shift in identity—from employee to portfolio professional. She had not quit. She had expanded.

Carla's moment is a small one, yet it captures a truth that many workers are only beginning to see. The AI-driven economy does not reward single bets. It rewards adaptable portfolios, layered skills, multiple channels of contribution, and relationships that compound over time. In other words, it rewards agency. And that agency belongs not only to solo creators or venture-funded founders but to teachers, administrators, tradespeople, analysts, civil servants, and anyone willing to reimagine the geometry of their working life.

But another story runs alongside hers. In a renovated warehouse in Leeds, a three-person marketing agency—two strategists and one designer—manages a client roster that once required a staff of twelve. Automated reporting handles their weekly analytics; prompt libraries generate early creative drafts; integrated dashboards collapse complexity. The time saved doesn't disappear. It is funnelled into client strategy, relationship-building, and higher-order planning. The team does not feel smaller. It feels sharper. The tools have shifted the gravity of their work from production to judgement.

These scenes are not outliers. They are early indicators of a structural transition: a labour market where productivity is no longer tied neatly to headcount, where careers become clusters rather than ladders, and where value pools tilt toward those who can combine human nuance with automated capability. Thriving within this environment requires more than technical facility. It requires an understanding of how to design one's economic life for resilience, autonomy, and leverage.

Across the next pages, this chapter asks a simple but unsettling question: what does it mean to build a fulfilling, durable working life when the shape of work itself is fluid? The question matters because many of the traditional anchors—the single employer, the linear promotion path, the fixed job description—are losing their grip. Automation doesn't merely reshape tasks. It reshapes incentives. It shifts the balance of power within teams. It widens the gap between those who can translate tools into outcomes and those who wait for instructions. It rewards individuals who can navigate uncertainty with curiosity rather than fear.

Portfolio careers form the first arc of this chapter. Not because everyone must become an entrepreneur, but because diversification—of income, of identity, of skill—reduces fragility. In a world where algorithms alter workflows overnight, a single professional identity becomes a single point of failure. The aim is not restlessness; it is rootedness with breadth. Carla's course illustrates this gently: she built a second stream without abandoning the first, using AI not to replace her craft but to multiply its reach.

Yet diversification alone is not enough. The real frontier of the AI-driven economy lies with small teams—two to five people—who wield tools with strategic intent. When a tiny firm automates reporting, integrates knowledge flows, or systematises creative processes, it does not merely save time. It reclaims attention. And attention is the scarce resource from which competitive advantage grows. These teams demonstrate a pattern that larger organisations struggle to emulate: operational systems that scale insight without scaling bureaucracy. Their advantage is not speed for its own sake but clarity—clarity about what to automate, what to own, and what to ignore.

But leverage has a counterweight: fairness. When tools amplify output, the question of equitable compensation becomes unavoidable. Who captures the gains when productivity surges? How should pay align with contribution when contribution itself is augmented? In newsrooms, this tension has already surfaced. After several outlets adopted automated summarisation in 2021, many reporters found their workload re-centred around investigative and analytical work. Some teams renegotiated beats to protect time for deeper reporting; others pushed for outcome-based metrics that recognised the comparative value of stories requiring human labour. These negotiations signal a broader shift: as automation handles volume, human worth is measured increasingly through judgement, originality, and ethical responsibility.

And then there is the geography of value. Technological change has a way of flattening some markets while sharpening others. The AI-driven economy is no exception. Not all value is global, and not all competition scales. A repair shop in Dundee, using AI diagnostics to shorten assessment times, wins not because it competes with a multinational car brand but because it pairs efficient triage with local trust. Customers return because the staff remember their name, their car, their worries. Local moats—relationships, reputation, reliability—remain powerful. When combined with well-deployed tools, they become nearly unassailable.

Threaded through these examples is a subtle motif: the hinge. Technology creates inflection points, moments where a small shift in behaviour unlocks a disproportionate change in outcome. A teacher posts a course. A trio automates weekly tasks. A newsroom redraws beats. A repair team integrates diagnostics. Every hinge begins with the same question: *What could I release, redesign, or reimagine if the tools took care of the mechanical work?* Every hinge ends with the same realisation: value flows toward those who act early, thoughtfully, and with clear boundaries.

This chapter stands at the intersection of economics and personal agency. Its argument is practical yet philosophical: thriving in an AI-driven economy is not a function of chasing every new tool. It is a practice of choosing: choosing where to diversify, choosing how to design small teams for disproportionate effectiveness, choosing how to negotiate fair pay for augmented work, and choosing when to build local advantage instead of chasing scale. The skill is not adoption. The skill is discernment.

As we move deeper into this chapter, the focus will widen from individual examples to systemic patterns. We will examine how risk can be controlled through time-boxed experiments; how micro-teams can build operating systems that punch above their size; how labour markets may rebalance around outcomes rather than hours; and how communities can weave technological capability into their identity rather than fear its encroachment. Always, the anchor will be the same: human agency amplified, not eclipsed, by intelligent systems.

And yet, a tension hums under the narrative—one worth carrying forward as you read. If the AI-driven economy rewards those who design their lives with intention, what happens to those who cling to inherited structures? If value tilts toward adaptability, how do we ensure that security does not evaporate? If tools expand possibility, who decides what counts as meaningful contribution?

The rest of the chapter will not resolve these questions fully. But it will give you the language, examples, and frameworks needed to navigate them with clarity. The hinges are already appearing. The challenge—and the opportunity—is deciding which ones you will turn.

Portfolio careers

At 19:27 on 14 September 2023, in a terraced house in Norwich, English teacher Carla Howard clicked "publish" on the first paid online course she had ever created. The course—*How to Read Fiction Like a Writer*—had taken shape over six weeks of late evenings. Carla had drafted her lessons with familiar care, but what made the project viable was a quiet shift in how she worked. She used an AI planning tool to organise modules, a language model to check phrasing and tighten examples, and a lightweight quiz generator to test comprehension. None of this replaced her judgement; it removed the friction that had deterred her from attempting such a project for years. By Sunday evening she saw her first £180 in enrolments. She told no one at school. She didn't need to. The point wasn't escape. It was expansion.

Carla's experience captures a pattern now spreading across professions that once assumed a single-track career. The AI-driven economy lowers the activation energy required to build a secondary craft—writing, consulting, tutoring, coding, illustrating, designing, researching—and to do it without abandoning a primary role. The pattern is neither a fad nor a promise of effortless income. It is, rather, a structural shift in how individuals can accumulate skills, relationships, and economic resilience. A portfolio career is no longer the preserve of freelancers or founders. It is increasingly the rational stance of any professional navigating volatility.

The motif that threads this subchapter is the anchor. A portfolio career is not drift across multiple identities, but a stable centre with multiple extensions. The anchor keeps a person grounded; the extensions generate optionality. Carla remains anchored in teaching. Her course is an extension—designed deliberately, bounded by time, and sheltered from catastrophic downside.

To see how this dynamic unfolds, begin with the mechanics of diversification. Show, name, explain, implication. Show: Carla devoted six hours per week to developing her course, constrained to evenings and early mornings. Name: this is a *time box*. Explain: time boxes limit exposure—she could explore without risking burnout or neglecting her primary role. Implication: structured experimentation reduces fear. It turns ambition into something testable.

A similar pattern appears in a different sector. In 2021, data analyst Joshua Patel at a telecoms firm in Birmingham began offering part-time analytics coaching to small charities. He used AI tools to automate data cleaning, prepare templates, and produce early drafts of visualisations. His anchor remained his full-time job; the extension was a modest consulting practice that generated £600–£800 per month. The visible behaviours—ring-fenced hours, transparent pricing, small pilot engagements—demonstrated how risk controls work in practice. He did not stretch himself thin. He stretched his capabilities.

Portfolio careers also shift how people learn. Instead of viewing professional development as a linear climb through a single ladder, individuals treat learning as layered accumulation. A skill gained in one stream reinforces the others. Carla's course sharpened her classroom instruction. Joshua's charity coaching improved his internal presentations. The exchange runs in both directions.

Historically, this layering was rare because the friction of creating new products or services was high. In 1999, when London schoolteacher Mary Hoare developed her GCSE revision book on poetry, she spent nearly two years preparing the manuscript, negotiating printer contracts, and handling distribution. Her anchor held, but the extension demanded heroic effort. Today, equivalent efforts take weeks. AI tools reduce drafting time, structure review cycles, and compress the distance between intent and output.

But diversification has limits. A counter-example illustrates the point. In 2022, a software engineer in Edinburgh attempted to launch five micro-projects simultaneously: a newsletter, a paid course, a productivity app, a design template pack, and a community forum. Each used AI tools for scaffolding. But without a single anchor or a clear sense of priority, the extensions cannibalised one another. The engineer abandoned all five within four months. The limitation is clear: tools may accelerate creation, but they cannot supply coherence. Reconcile the counter-example by restating the principle: portfolio careers require anchoring, sequencing, and scope. Without these, the portfolio becomes chaos.

Anchoring clarifies identity. Sequencing prevents overload. Scope boundaries stop an experiment from metastasising into obligation.

Consider anchoring more closely. It is not merely psychological. It is economic. A stable anchor—a professional role, a client retainer, a recurring teaching assignment—subsidises experimentation. It allows someone like Carla to accept early income variability because her mortgage, bills, and pension contributions travel through the steady stream of her salaried job. The anchor funds the extension. Without an anchor, diversification becomes gambling.

Sequencing, in turn, manages uncertainty. A common pattern among successful portfolio professionals is the "single experiment per quarter" rule. Joshua tested his analytics coaching in March 2021, paused to review outcomes, then expanded cautiously in July. By contrast, the Edinburgh engineer tested five ideas in parallel and failed to gather meaningful feedback. Sequencing converts possibility into signal. It preserves attention.

Scope boundaries prevent runaway commitments. Carla capped her course at four modules. She refused requests for a live cohort until she had taught the material once. Joshua refused custom analytics projects that required bespoke modelling. These behaviours give substance to the abstraction of "risk management".

The motif of the anchor returns when examining identity. Portfolio careers challenge the long-standing Western belief that a person is defined by a singular professional role. This belief was already fraying in the early 2000s as gig work and hybrid roles emerged. The AI-driven economy accelerates the breakdown. Identity becomes composite. But composite identity is not fragmentation. It is a form of resilience. When one extension falters, the anchor holds.

Examples from institutional contexts underscore this. In 2020, the BBC allowed several reporters to develop side projects—podcasts, books, training courses—under structured agreements. The anchor was the newsroom. The extensions were controlled: time-limited, conflict-checked, and publicly disclosed. Reporters sharpened their craft; the organisation benefited from stronger voices. But the boundaries mattered. BBC editorial guidelines required that any external work avoid duplicating internal assignments. The anchor stayed firm.

In academia, portfolio careers have long existed through consulting, writing, and speaking. But the role of AI tools now changes the pace. In 2023, historian Maya Jasanoff at Harvard used transcription and large-scale text analysis to accelerate archival reviews. Faster data gathering allowed her to accept external projects—curatorial advisory, short courses—without harming her research trajectory. The visible behaviour is the same as in Norwich or Birmingham: the anchor remains; the extension expands through well-designed workflows.

The counter-limitation: portfolio careers risk eroding rest. When extensions creep into leisure time, burnout follows. A 2022 study by the UK's Chartered Institute of Personnel and Development found that workers with multiple income streams reported higher satisfaction but also higher exhaustion when boundaries were weak. Reconciliation lies in the discipline of sabbath weeks—scheduled intervals where extensions pause and only the anchor remains. Successful portfolio professionals rest their extensions to maintain their anchors.

At the structural level, portfolio careers reflect a shift away from single-employer dependency and toward personal economic ecosystems. The inputs—skills, tools, networks, reputation—compound over time. The outputs—income, autonomy, resilience—diversify. The risk profile changes: instead of relying on one employer's fortunes, a worker distributes exposure across multiple endeavours.

But a portfolio is not a hedge fund. It is a lived pattern of attention. Where the financial world diversifies through assets, individuals diversify through roles. The roles need harmony.

As this subchapter reaches its final movement, the motif of the anchor sharpens into a practical dilemma. Carla refreshes her course page. Joshua closes a charity project. Both have expanded their professional range without severing their base. Yet each now faces the same forward test: how much extension is enough? When does diversification strengthen identity, and when does it stretch it thin? When does the anchor support, and when does it constrain?

A portfolio career flourishes not at the point of maximum variety, but at the point of coherent multiplicity. And so the question that remains—quiet, insistent—is this: in designing your own professional life, what will you choose as your anchor, and which extensions will you allow it to carry?

Small teams, big leverage

At 08:42 on 6 February 2024, in a converted loft above Camden Lock, the three-person agency BrightFold delivered a weekly analytics report to its largest client, a retail chain expanding across the Midlands. The surprising part was not the punctuality. It was that the team had spent just seventeen minutes preparing a package that used to consume more than six hours. The agency's director, Megan Lewis, had built an automated reporting pipeline that ingested campaign data, generated summaries, drafted slide outlines, and surfaced anomalies for manual review. The time saved that Tuesday—five and a half hours—was spent probing the client's stalled loyalty programme. By Friday, BrightFold had redesigned the rewards ladder and won a contract extension worth £28,000. Three people had produced the output of a small department. Their advantage lay not in numbers, but in what they chose to automate, standardise, and amplify.

The pattern is replicable. When small teams commit to a coherent operating system—one that treats tools as structural rather than ornamental—they unlock capacities once reserved for much larger firms. The unit of analysis is not headcount. It is throughput per person. And when AI systems compress the distance between intent and execution, a group of two-to-five committed individuals can outperform organisations ten times their size. The image that threads through this subchapter is the flywheel: a compact mechanism that stores energy, requires little to maintain momentum, and accelerates dramatically once initial resistance falls. Small teams thrive when their flywheels spin without friction.

To understand why this shift matters, start by showing a behaviour rather than naming a theory. BrightFold's reporting workflow in 2021 involved exporting CSV files, reformatting tables in Excel, copying charts into PowerPoint, and rewriting highlights by hand. Name: this is manual data wrangling. Explain: each step consumed attention and introduced error risk, slowing the team's ability to interpret results. Implication: the team had no space for higher-order analysis because operational overhead dominated the week. In 2024 the behaviour changed. Automation handled formatting and first-draft interpretation. The bottleneck disappeared, revealing an uncomfortable but liberating truth: the team had been spending the bulk of its energy on work that did not require human judgement.

A second example illustrates the structural nature of leverage. At the software studio Monocle Labs in Manchester, co-founders David Lee and Sarah Collings built their internal "OpsFrame" in late 2022: a lightweight system integrating GitHub, Notion, and a set of AI-assisted code review scripts. The metrics were stark. Average pull-request review time dropped from thirty-two hours to seven. Bug regression rates fell by 18 percent (GitHub Insights, 2023). With only four developers, Monocle Labs delivered client builds at a pace that allowed them to compete with firms three times their size. The visible behaviour—rapid feedback cycles—was the signature of a well-designed flywheel. Once the cycle ran smoothly, every additional feature pushed the wheel faster.

Yet not every small team succeeds. A counter-example is instructive. In 2021, a Brighton-based creative duo attempted to adopt five new digital tools in a single month—project management software, an AI writing assistant, an invoicing platform, an automated asset tagging system, and a scheduling bot. The result was paralysis. Tools collided, notifications multiplied, and both partners abandoned the experiment out of frustration. Their limitation was not ambition. It was absence of an operating system. Reconciliation lies in design discipline: small teams cannot absorb tool proliferation; they require intentional sequencing and clear boundaries.

The principle is simple but rarely practised. A team must first commit to a core workflow that determines how information enters, moves through, and leaves the organisation. Then tools reinforce the workflow rather than disrupt it. BrightFold's reporting flywheel, for example, rests on a single canonical data repository and a defined review sequence. Monocle Labs' engineering flywheel relies on clear ownership of modules and standardised prompts for automated code checks. The motif repeats: discipline stabilises the flywheel.

A deeper implication emerges when examining why tiny teams can surpass larger rivals. Coordination cost rises with headcount. In a thirty-person department, communication pathways exceed four hundred. In a four-person team, there are six. This mathematical asymmetry means that every automation added to a small team displaces relatively more coordination overhead than it would in a large one. When BrightFold automated reporting, they did not merely save hours; they collapsed intra-team communication that once revolved around drafting, reviewing, and reconciling slide decks. The flywheel spun faster because fewer hands touched each stage.

But efficiency alone is not the point. Leverage is meaningful only when it is reinvested. The strongest small teams convert saved hours into deeper client insight, product refinement, or strategic repositioning. BrightFold used their Tuesday windfall to identify a hidden pattern: the retailer's loyalty sign-ups dipped in stores where checkout queues averaged eight minutes. The observation required human interpretation. Tools accelerated the legwork; humans delivered the insight. The visible behaviour—shifting from administrative work to hypothesis generation—shows how small teams translate automation into advantage.

To see the broader pattern, consider the architectural studio FieldNorth in Glasgow. With just two architects and one technician, they built an AI-assisted planning review tool in 2023 that flagged regulatory constraints for each site proposal. Local approvals moved faster. Client iterations dropped from six rounds to two. The time saved went into materials research and community engagement. FieldNorth's fees rose accordingly; they could charge for judgement rather than drafting. The daily behaviour that mattered was the morning "constraint scan" ritual: a ten-minute AI-assisted check, followed by a human interpretation session. The flywheel again: reduced operational drag, increased creative depth, repeat.

Yet a limitation remains. Tool-driven acceleration can push teams into overcommitment. The temptation to accept more clients or launch more features grows when workflows become fluid. But overextension breaks the flywheel. Monocle Labs learned this in late 2023 when they accepted three overlapping contracts and found that while code reviews were fast, strategic planning was not. They paused new work for six weeks to rebuild spacing rules into their operating system—fixed delivery windows, capped concurrent projects, and a mandatory weekly planning hour. They recovered because they restored slack.

Slack is not the opposite of efficiency. It is its precondition. Every small team that endures builds margins into its operating system: buffers for unexpected delays, windows for exploratory work, guardrails for quality control. Automation without slack produces brittle speed. Automation with slack produces durable leverage.

This tension leads to the next claim: tooling is not the differentiator; operating systems are. BrightFold's pipeline could be copied by any agency. Monocle Labs' code scripts are not proprietary. What cannot be copied easily is the cultural commitment to maintaining a coherent flywheel. The behaviour is visible in meetings, not software logs. At BrightFold, Tuesday mornings are sacred: one hour of strategy, no reporting talk allowed. At Monocle Labs, code merges pause at 15:00 each Thursday to allow cross-team review. These rituals harden the operating system.

Examples from outside technology reinforce the principle. In 2022, the three-person non-profit advisory team at CivicBench in Liverpool implemented an AI-assisted grant scanning system. The system read hundreds of pages of eligibility criteria and surfaced opportunities suitable for local charities. The team reduced their research time by 70 percent, but the crucial gain lay elsewhere. They reallocated the hours to relationship-building with small community groups that struggled to articulate their needs. The flywheel here was not speed but trust. Automation created room for human engagement.

Still, a counter-pressure arises: tool ecosystems change rapidly. A system built in March 2023 may require restructuring by December. Operating systems must therefore adapt without breaking. The best small teams commit to quarterly reviews of their flywheel—testing assumptions, pruning tools, refining rituals. Adaptation becomes part of the operating system itself. Stability is not static; it is maintained.

As the subchapter moves to its final tension, return to the motif of the flywheel. BrightFold's momentum depends on their ability to keep drag low and direction clear. Monocle Labs relies on structured cadence. CivicBench depends on rituals that preserve trust. The central dilemma emerges: when should a small team accelerate its flywheel, and when should it resist acceleration to preserve coherence?

The forward test is demanding. What part of the workflow deserves automation next? Which human activities produce disproportionate insight? Which rituals safeguard quality? And most importantly: at what point does adding speed threaten the very strategic depth that gives the team its edge?

Small teams will continue to outperform—when their flywheels spin with intention, not haste. The unresolved question you must confront is this: if your team of two, three, or five could reclaim five hours tomorrow, where would you reinvest that time—and what would that choice reveal about the future you are trying to build?

Fair pay for augmented work

At 09:15 on 3 October 2023, in the open-plan newsroom of the *Bristol Herald*, senior reporter Amina Clarke refreshed the internal dashboard that now generated automated story summaries. The system, introduced quietly in August, scraped police logs, council notices, and court filings, producing brief, publishable updates in under two minutes. In September, it had drafted over 430 such summaries—work that once absorbed the mornings of three junior reporters. The concrete outcome was obvious: more output, delivered faster, with fewer hands. Yet when Amina met her editor, Mark Ellery, later that morning, she raised a blunt question: if the newsroom could produce twice as many updates with the same staff, what happened to the value of the deeper work—investigations that required days, relationships, and judgement? Her beat had not shrunk, but her time had. "If we don't renegotiate," she said, "this just becomes speed without purpose." Mark agreed. By November, the *Herald* reallocated beats, protected investigative hours, and redesigned its pay structure to reward the outcomes humans still uniquely delivered.

The case anchors a wider tension. When tools compress routine labour, output rises, but contributions shift. Automation has lowered the cost of summarising, tagging, transcribing, and organising information. Yet none of these activities define the highest-value human work in knowledge industries. The *Herald* faced the question sooner than most: what is fair pay when augmentation multiplies throughput but does not distribute recognition? The newsroom's renegotiation shows the gravity of this shift. Visible behaviour changed first—journalists filed longer pieces, not summaries. The next move required naming what had changed: automation had displaced baseline production, not journalistic craft. The implication was unavoidable: compensation needed to follow contribution, not volume.

To understand how automation reshapes pay, start by observing how augmentation alters workflows. At the *Herald*, before August 2023, a reporter spent roughly 90 minutes turning raw notes from police reports into a coherent 250-word update. After the automated summariser went live, that time fell to under ten minutes. The visible behaviour—reduced drafting time—reveals the shift. Now name the structural change: summarisation had become commodified. Explain: the value of a reporter's labour no longer came from compression of information but from narrative framing and source validation. Implication: pay tied to volume would distort incentives by rewarding what machines already did well.

A second example reinforces this pattern. In April 2022, the legal firm Carter & Holt in Leeds adopted an AI-assisted evidence classifier. Before deployment, paralegals spent an average of 22 hours per case categorising documents. After deployment, classification time dropped to five hours (internal compliance audit, Carter & Holt, 2022). But the partners did not reduce staff. They reassigned paralegals to client interviews and case analysis, raising billable utilisation by 18 percent without extending hours. The behaviour—paralegals spending more time interpreting rather than sorting—signalled a revaluation of their role. The firm revised pay bands the following year to reflect complexity handled, not hours logged. Their flywheel—more insight, more client confidence, stronger case preparation—depended on rewarding judgement.

Still, not all organisations respond responsibly. A credible counter-example illustrates the stakes. In 2021, a regional media conglomerate implemented an AI transcription tool that reduced interview processing time by 70 percent. Rather than preserving the reclaimed hours for deeper reporting, management increased output targets for staff writers by 40 percent with no salary adjustment. The result was predictable: quality fell, corrections rose, and two senior journalists left within six months. The limitation here is not the tool; it is the failure to match expectations with contribution. Reconciliation lies in the logic the *Herald* embraced: when augmentation frees capacity, choose to reinvest it in depth rather than dilute it through pressure.

The central concept running through this subchapter is the scale: a symbol of balance used not only to weigh goods but to weigh fairness. Whenever augmentation alters workflows, the scale shifts. An organisation must measure not only output but origin—what part of the outcome stems from human judgement, and what derives from machine acceleration. The *Herald* measured by analysing three datasets: average article length before and after automation, the proportion of unique sources per story, and the number of investigative leads generated weekly. The metrics showed that when summaries were automated, journalists spent 22 percent more time on interviews and 17 percent more time on data verification. In the revised pay model, investigative contributions carried explicit weighting.

But fair pay cannot rest solely on internal measurement. It must consider bargaining power. Show this in behaviour: Amina and her colleagues prepared a dossier summarising how their responsibilities had shifted. Name the practice: structured bargaining. Explain: workers articulate the specific ways augmentation has changed their contribution and propose compensation aligned with verifiable outcomes—leads generated, corrections avoided, exclusives earned. Implication: bargaining becomes evidence-led rather than sentiment-led. The conversation moves from "we feel undervalued" to "here are the measurable results only we can produce."

A second named example sharpens the point. In November 2023, at the healthcare provider St. Matthew's Trust in Birmingham, ward managers negotiated new staffing allocations after an AI-supported triage tool reduced average nurse handover time by 15 minutes per shift (Trust Operational Review, 2023). Nurses argued that while handover time fell, complexity rose: they now spent more minutes explaining algorithmic recommendations to patients and families. The Trust accepted this claim because it was documented through time-and-motion studies. The behaviour—slower conversations with anxious families—was visible and measurable. Compensation adjustments followed, not because nurses produced more volume, but because they carried more emotional and interpretive labour.

Yet augmentation can sharpen inequality if left unchecked. Teams whose work is easily measurable—coders, analysts, editors—can often evidence their contribution. Those whose value is relational may struggle. Consider the case of a community liaison officer at a housing charity in Newcastle. Automation reduced her administrative burden by 40 percent, but her actual contribution—mediating tenant disputes, de-escalating tensions, fostering trust—rarely produced numeric indicators. Without explicit frameworks, her value risked eroding. This limitation exposes a deeper problem: fairness requires metrics that honour complexity. The reconciliation is not simple. Organisations must record behaviours that illustrate relational contribution—conflict resolution time, complaint volumes, follow-up satisfaction scores—but remain cautious about crude scoring.

This leads to a broader implication: augmented workplaces need competence-aware pay, not automation-blind pay. When tools lift some tasks but raise expectations for others, compensation must map to the rising frontier of human contribution. The *Herald*, Carter & Holt, and St. Matthew's adopted this principle in different forms, but each centred one question: what value did humans create that machines did not amplify automatically?

At this point, the scale motif returns. The balance must consider three forces: output accelerated by tools, outcomes produced by humans, and expectations set by management. When these forces align, morale strengthens. When misaligned, resentment accumulates. People sense when their contribution has been miscounted. They know when the organisation's scales skew.

But measurement alone cannot solve bargaining. Teams require confidence to articulate their contribution. At the *Herald*, journalists rehearsed a simple structure: describe the changed workflow, show the new behaviour, quantify the outcome, propose a standard. This was not a list of demands; it was a narrative with evidence. Bargaining succeeds when both sides see the same picture.

Still, unresolved tensions remain. How should organisations handle augmentation that raises output but lowers cognitive strain? If a summarisation tool reduces effort yet raises volume, should pay rise, fall, or stay constant? What matters more: effort, skill, or outcome? And how should organisations prevent augmentation from masking overwork? When the *Herald* automated summaries, some managers initially suggested writers take on additional beats. Only Amina's intervention prevented overload.

The practical dilemma is unavoidable: fair pay in an augmented workplace cannot rely on legacy metrics like hours or volume. It must prioritise contribution that remains scarce. Yet scarcity shifts. Narrative framing, investigative tenacity, judgement under uncertainty—these can be amplified but not replaced by automation. Workers must document these contributions. Organisations must honour them.

This brings the scale motif to its final form: fairness rests on transparency. When organisations share how augmentation distributes effort and impact, pay negotiations become clearer. When they hide it, trust erodes.

The unresolved question sits with you now. If a tool tomorrow reduced the mundane part of your work by half, and raised your capacity for the demanding part, what evidence would you bring to show that your contribution had grown—not shrunk—because of it?

Local advantage

At 14:07 on 11 May 2023, in a narrow side street off Mansfield Road in Nottingham, the owner of Riley's Auto Service, Daniel Riley, ran an AI-assisted diagnostic on a ten-year-old Ford Focus. The customer, a local courier named Kate Singh, needed the car back before the evening rush. The tool flagged three plausible faults in under ninety seconds. But Daniel did what he had always done: he walked to the car, listened to the idle, checked the wear pattern on the front tyres, and asked Kate about the past week's routes. The concrete outcome was modest but telling. The AI suggested replacing the ignition coil—a correct but incomplete answer. Daniel identified a secondary issue: a mounting bracket that had loosened after a series of potholes on Gregory Boulevard. He fixed both problems in under an hour. By the time Kate drove away, she had booked her next service. The shop's combination of rapid diagnostics and intimate local knowledge created a moat no app could match. The repair was faster because of the tool. The trust was earned because of Daniel.

The case captures a tension that structures the entire argument: automation globalises capability, but value remains local. AI diagnostics, whether in cars, appliances, or infrastructure, draw on global data. But people do not build lives in global averages; they build them in specific streets, cultures, and relationships. The repair shop's competitive edge did not come from possessing an advanced model—it came from embedding the model into a web of relationships, tacit knowledge, and community history. Daniel knew the roads; he knew which models struggled with moisture after a wet winter; he knew his customers' time pressures. The local advantage sat not in the tool but in *how* it was situated.

To understand this dynamic, begin with behaviour, not abstraction. A customer walks into Riley's Auto Service. She is greeted by name. Her work schedule is known. Her typical mileage is known. The visible behaviour is recognition. Name the underlying capability: relational continuity. Explain: knowing the patterns of an individual customer changes every subsequent interaction, from diagnosing faults to estimating turnaround time. Implication: when automation speeds up the mechanical parts of service, relational knowledge becomes a compound asset—it reduces friction at the very moment tools reduce technical labour.

A second named example shows the pattern in a different field. In November 2022, at Anderson & Co., a three-solicitor practice in Dundee, the partners implemented an AI tool that drafted first-pass contract summaries. Drafting time fell by 60 percent (internal workflow audit, Anderson & Co., 2023). Yet their competitive advantage did not come from speed alone. Their lead solicitor, Fiona Anderson, invested the reclaimed hours in client conversations—guiding new small business owners through regulatory complexities specific to Dundee's council policies. Her signature move was to walk clients through examples from local cases: which cafés struggled with late-night permits on Perth Road, which landlords renegotiated leases after footfall dipped in 2021. Her behaviour created confidence that no generic summary could replicate. Her value rested in place-specific judgement.

But local advantage has limits. A counter-example clarifies this. In 2021, a high-street electronics repair chain attempted to expand into York with a heavily automated service desk. Diagnostics ran quickly. Turnaround time was technically sound. Yet within nine months the branch closed. Customer surveys (York Consumer Panel, 2022) showed the same criticism: the staff rotated frequently, did not recognise regulars, and misread seasonal patterns—such as the flood-prone months that caused recurring issues with home routers. The limitation was not the toolset. It was the absence of embedded local knowledge. Reconciliation emerges when we recognise that automation can compress technical variance but exacerbates cultural variance. Where global capability spreads evenly, local interpretation becomes the differentiator.

This leads to the motif that threads through the subchapter: the map and the street. Automation provides the map—wide, consistent, and generalisable. Human expertise occupies the street—imperfect, contingent, and specific. The map shows what is statistically likely. The street shows what actually happens. When Daniel listened to Kate's engine, he was not rejecting the AI's suggestion; he was reading the street-level evidence. And when Fiona advised her clients, she was interpreting the regulatory map through the realities of local dynamics.

To understand why place still matters, dissect the structure of trust. Trust is often named but rarely grounded. In practice, trust is a sequence of observable behaviours: accurate estimates, remembered context, honest triage, and visible care. In Daniel's shop, trust appears when he calls a customer ten minutes before closing to confirm a fix rather than letting it drift to tomorrow. In Fiona's office, trust appears when she outlines the two paths a contract might take under Dundee's specific enforcement patterns, not just the theoretical options an AI tool presents. These behaviours anchor expectations. They create a moat that is relational, not technological.

Two additional named examples reinforce how local moats form. In July 2023, the community pharmacy at Rosehill in Oxford implemented a medication-interaction checker. The tool caught potential conflicts faster than manual review. But pharmacist Nisha Patel noticed a recurring pattern the model missed: during Ramadan, customers' dosing schedules shifted dramatically, increasing the risk of side effects in the evenings. Her behaviour—asking patients about fasting—transformed the raw diagnostic into safe practice. The model held the map. She walked the street.

Another example comes from the hospitality sector. At Café Solstice in Falmouth, the owner, Luis Moreno, used AI to forecast demand based on weather patterns and local events. The predictions were often correct. But his decision to increase Sunday staffing was based not on the system's suggestion but on a local tradition: families leaving the harbour after choir practice tended to stop by for tea if the temperature fell below 12°C. This behaviour repeated every winter. The forecast model did not know the choir schedule; Luis did. And so the café operated smoothly while competitors struggled with unpredictable footfall.

Automation amplifies gaps between those who understand their local terrain and those who treat tools as substitutes for context. This tension becomes sharper as more tools become commodified. Diagnostic models become cheaper. Forecasting models become widely available. Recommendation systems proliferate. The global map becomes more detailed, yet more generic. The advantage shifts to those who interpret the map with precision.

But local advantage is not just knowledge; it is responsiveness. When Daniel resolved Kate's repair in under an hour, speed mattered because it matched her shift deadlines. When Fiona advised business owners, her value lay partly in tailoring contracts to the constraints of Dundee's micro-economy. When Nisha interpreted dosing risks, she aligned care with cultural rhythms. Local advantage emerges when interpretation meets timing.

One might argue that large platforms can simply ingest more local data, closing this gap. It is a credible concern. But platforms face constraints. They do not experience place. They do not inhabit local relationships. They model probability; they do not witness nuance. Consider a rideshare algorithm that learns traffic patterns in Birmingham. It may predict congestion accurately. But it will not know that a particular junction becomes chaotic when the local secondary school hosts evening sports events. Only drivers know. And drivers act. The limitation of data-driven local inference is that it lacks lived context. The reconciliation is simple: global systems can assist local actors, but cannot replace them where judgement depends on situated experience.

This reveals another layer: community memory. Local advantage accumulates when people remember what happened last year, and the year before, and the year before that. Daniel remembers the potholes that the council failed to fix. Fiona remembers which landlord shifted terms during lockdown. Nisha remembers who struggled with dosing last Ramadan. Luis remembers the choir pattern. Community memory is a reservoir of implicit data. Automation cannot easily capture it because it exists in conversations, relationships, and patterns that never produce structured inputs.

This means that local moats deepen through repeated interactions. Behaviour compounds. A customer returns not because diagnostics are fast, but because they feel understood. A client returns not because a contract was summarised quickly, but because the advice reflected local realities. Local advantage is built slowly but defended strongly.

The deeper implication is philosophical: automation's global reach highlights the importance of rootedness. When tools flatten the technical differences between providers, what remains scarce is the *fit* between service and circumstance. Fit cannot be globalised. Fit is local.

The scale of local advantage also matters for economic resilience. In mid-2023, the repair shop faced competition from a national service chain advertising ultra-fast AI diagnostics. Daniel's business grew nonetheless. His turnaround time beat the chain's because he prioritised walk-ins from nearby couriers, many of whom preferred immediate fixes to formal bookings. His judgement aligned with local need. The chain's map was accurate. Daniel's street was decisive.

Now the motif returns: the map and the street. The map extends reach, but only the street ensures relevance. The future of small enterprises, neighbourhood clinics, independent agencies, and community services will hinge on this interplay. Automation will continue to expand the map's resolution. Local practitioners must strengthen their presence on the street.

The unresolved tension surfaces here. If automation keeps improving, will local judgement remain differentiating or become another layer for models to mimic? Or will rootedness grow more important as global systems converge? The forward test is demanding: which parts of your work draw on place, relationship, and memory—and which parts merely follow the map?

Chapter 5
Ethics Without Paralysis

At 08:32 on a grey March morning in 2023, the hiring team at Brookhaven Instruments sat in a windowless meeting room in Cambridge, staring at two résumés that looked identical—same degree, same experience, same certifications—except for the names. One CV belonged to a candidate called Daniel; the other to someone called Rehan. When the team ran both profiles through their recently installed screening model, Daniel was recommended for interview with a confident green tick, while Rehan was flagged amber. The silence in the room was sharp. They ran the test again. The result repeated. A tool purchased to increase fairness had quietly encoded the opposite. By lunchtime, the team had begun a counterfactual audit—swapping names, rearranging work histories, probing the murky edges of the model's logic—and by late afternoon, they had traced the issue to a training dataset skewed by historical hiring patterns. The discovery did not make them anti-automation. It made them more deliberate. They had learned the first lesson of ethical deployment: systems replicate patterns unless someone stops them.

That small moment—two CVs, one uncomfortable discrepancy—captures the defining tension of our age. Intelligent systems move fast, scale silently, and weave themselves into decisions we once believed were firmly human. Organisations deploy them to accelerate diagnosis, hiring, routing, triage, or surveillance. But speed brings shadows: bias that hides in statistical grooves; privacy diluted by enthusiasm for more data; safety boundaries stretched by ambition; dignity worn thin by metrics with no memory of the people they measure. Ethics, then, is not a philosophical footnote but an operational discipline. It is a form of craft. And like any craft, it has tools, habits, rituals, and checks.

What this chapter asks is simple but demanding: how do individuals and institutions act responsibly without freezing in fear? There is a common misconception that ethics slows everything down, that oversight belongs to committees and binders, that caution is the enemy of innovation. Yet the stories that unfold across sectors tell a different truth. A small clinic in Glasgow, revising its patient intake forms, removed half its fields—not as a gesture of minimalism, but because every unnecessary question invited risk. Encryption became the default. Access logs became visible to staff. Paradoxically, these constraints improved service: patients received faster care because staff navigated cleaner, narrower data environments. Ethics sharpened, rather than blurred, the work.

That pattern repeats in more complex settings. A British drone-mapping service preparing to scale across the Midlands found itself grappling with a deceptively difficult question: where should its aircraft *never* fly? The aviation regulators had supplied guidelines; the engineering team had built sophisticated failsafes; yet the moral heart of the matter lay elsewhere. It required a conversation about boundaries—not generic risk zones but specific, place-bound decisions: avoiding wildlife sanctuaries in winter, steering clear of school grounds regardless of legal allowances, agreeing to abort missions when winds exceeded a threshold defined not by marketing promises but by engineering reality. They built a safety case, translated it into a daily checklist, and enforced it. As a result, they grew with fewer incidents and stronger trust.

And then there is the call centre on the outskirts of Manchester—a place where monitoring is nearly as old as the industry itself. In 2022 its leadership implemented an AI-driven scoring tool that analysed tone, pace, turn-taking, and even the pauses in conversation. The system rated calls, identifying moments when customers grew anxious or frustrated. But instead of hiding the model behind managerial dashboards, the centre chose the braver path: they published the scoring logic for all employees, invited questions, and established opt-out protections for sensitive cases. Complaints fell. Attrition softened. Staff said they felt treated as adults. By lifting the veil, the organisation underscored a principle that threads through ethical practice: dignity is inseparable from transparency.

These examples point to a larger story that frames the chapter ahead. Ethics is not a brake—it is a steering system. It helps organisations travel faster in the right direction rather than fast wherever gravity pulls. The question is not whether bias, privacy risks, or safety threats exist; they do, and they always will. The question is whether we build habits that reveal them early, mechanisms that address them plainly, and cultures that refuse to ignore uncomfortable signals. The tools are not exotic: counterfactual tests to catch bias; data minimisation to reduce risk; checklists that articulate boundaries; norms that make dignity visible.

But there is a deeper thread running beneath the practicalities. Intelligent systems alter power. They shift decision-making from visible human judgement to invisible statistical inference. They distribute responsibility across designers, deployers, and users. They tempt leaders to attribute their choices to "what the model said," as if agency dissolves into code. Ethics, then, is not only about better models. It is about preserving human accountability in environments where machines speak with increasing fluency.

This raises profound questions that cannot be postponed. When an algorithm rejects a job applicant, who explains the decision? When a predictive model misses a pattern that a human could have seen, who absorbs the consequences? When a safety boundary is crossed by a system that has no intuition of harm, who decides how the next boundary is drawn? These are not abstract dilemmas for regulators alone. They belong to managers, clinicians, engineers, operators—anyone who supervises or interacts with automated processes.

The chapter also asks you to consider the emotional dimension of ethical practice. People do not resist automation out of ignorance; they resist because they fear invisibility. When work becomes mediated by metrics, they worry that the richness of their contribution will be flattened. When decisions are delegated to opaque systems, they fear that recourse will evaporate. When surveillance expands, they fear they will be judged without context. Ethics without paralysis means recognising these fears not as obstacles but as signals: indicators of where systems must be adjusted, explained, constrained, or redesigned.

Yet something subtler sits alongside these anxieties. Intelligent systems can also protect dignity when used well. A hiring tool can flag inconsistencies that shield candidates from arbitrary prejudice. A privacy-by-design workflow can protect vulnerable patients from data misuse. A safety checklist can prevent corners from being cut by people under pressure. Ethical practice, at its best, does not merely prevent harm; it enables confidence.

As we move toward the close of this introductory movement, two motifs surface that will accompany the chapter: the mirror and the margin. Every automated system is a mirror; it reflects the data and decisions that shaped it. Every deployment creates a margin—an edge where risks concentrate, where oversight matters most, where dignity can be strengthened or thinned. Ethics without paralysis requires learning to inspect both: to look into the mirror without denial, and to fortify the margin without delay.

The chapters ahead will explore how organisations can build bias tests into daily routines, how privacy minimisation sharpens decision-making, how safety boundaries become rituals, and how dignity becomes a design constraint rather than a retrospective apology. The stakes are high. Intelligent systems promise scale and speed, but without ethics they corrode trust, compress autonomy, and amplify old structural imbalances. Navigating this terrain requires courage, clarity, and a willingness to confront what automated processes reveal about our own blind spots.

The tension that remains is productive. How do you maintain velocity without sacrificing care? How do you build systems that serve people without diminishing them? How do you protect the vulnerable without halting innovation? These are not questions with neat, universal answers. But they are the questions that must shape our next moves.

Turn the page with these questions in mind. The real work begins at the point where principles meet practice—where ethical intention must become operational habit, and where intelligent systems must be taught, firmly and continually, to serve the human future we choose.

Bias and oversight

At 10:46 on 18 April 2023, in the headquarters of Brookhaven Instruments on Hills Road in Cambridge, the hiring team sat before a projected spreadsheet that made everyone uneasy. Two résumés had been submitted the previous evening for a data analyst role. Same degree from the University of Manchester. Same two-year internship at the same logistics firm. Same certifications in SQL and Python. The only differences were the names: Daniel Roberts and Rehan Qureshi. When the team ran both profiles through their new screening model, installed that February, Daniel received a strong green endorsement. Rehan received a muted amber. The disparity seemed absurdly stark given the mirrorlike similarity of their histories. Someone suggested a rerun. Someone else suggested swapping names. Within minutes, the amber and green switched places. The room went quiet. What was meant to accelerate fairness had revealed a problem the team could not ignore.

The moment felt small—just two files, just two scores—but it exposed a larger truth: algorithms replicate patterns unless deliberately interrupted. The system had been trained on a decade of historical hiring data, and that history, like most institutional histories, contained its own skews. The machine had reproduced the grooves of past preferences, not the merits of present candidates. The motif of this subchapter—the mirror—arrives early. Automated systems reflect whatever they are shown, and when the reflection distorts, people must notice the angle.

To understand the mechanics of bias, start with behaviour rather than principle. Brookhaven's team did something concrete: they ran counterfactual résumés. They changed names, rearranged sequences, removed addresses. This is the daily craft of oversight. Name the technique: counterfactual testing. Explain its purpose: to reveal whether a model's output depends on variables that should be irrelevant to the task. Implication: without such tests, organisations may move forward with blind confidence, unaware that their tools encode inherited mistakes.

A second case shows the same pattern in a different domain. In November 2022, at Riverside Finance in Leeds, compliance officers reviewed credit approvals after integrating a risk assessment model that had been procured from an external vendor. A quarterly audit revealed that applicants from postcodes LS11 and LS12 were being rejected at a rate nearly 19 percent higher than those from LS2 and LS3, even after controlling for income and credit history (Riverside Compliance Report, 2023). The visible behaviour—a geographically clustered rejection pattern—prompted further tests. Name the finding: geographic proxy bias. Explain: the model had absorbed correlations between postcode, property value, and repayment rates, then amplified them. Implication: if organisations do not examine outputs with local knowledge, automated systems may entrench patterns that would be illegal or unethical if done intentionally.

Yet a credible counter-example reminds us that bias detection is rarely straightforward. In 2021, a recruitment startup in London attempted to correct for gender bias in its engineering-screening model by stripping names and pronouns. But despite the anonymisation, disparities persisted. The reason, discovered only after a forensic audit, was subtle: the structure of work histories—shorter tenures, role titles, patterns of parental leave—served as indirect identifiers. The limitation shows that naive "removal of sensitive fields" is inadequate. Reconciliation comes through a broader lesson: fair systems require scrutiny of the entire representational landscape, not just individual columns in a dataset.

How does oversight become operational rather than symbolic? Begin with the mirror again. Bias is rarely visible within the code; it emerges in the effects. Teams must measure behaviours. In Brookhaven's case, the measurable behaviour was the model's inconsistent scoring when names changed. In Riverside's case, it was the postcode differential. Oversight grows from patterns documented, not suspicions voiced. The flow is consistent: observe, test, document, escalate.

Escalation matters because bias often hides at the organisational edges. A junior recruiter notices anomalies but hesitates to raise them. A data scientist spots skew but assumes it is noise. Oversight fails when responsibility disperses. Successful teams designate an escalation path: who is told, when, and with what evidence. Brookhaven wrote theirs the week after the CV incident: any hiring anomaly must be logged, replicated, and sent directly to the head of People Analytics within twenty-four hours. This was not bureaucracy; it was accountability.

Bias also lives in assumptions that remain untested. Consider a case from health diagnostics. In January 2023, the Royal Infirmary of Edinburgh piloted an AI tool to support triage nurses in identifying sepsis risk. Initial results seemed promising. But after two weeks, nurses noticed a worrying pattern: patients who spoke English as a second language were being under-prioritised. The behaviour—slower escalation for multilingual patients—triggered an internal study. The model relied heavily on specific phrasing of symptoms as recorded in triage notes, unintentionally disadvantaging those whose speech patterns differed. The hospital halted deployment until a revised feature set could reduce linguistic dependence. The implication is uncomfortable but essential: bias is often introduced through the subtle interaction between human documentation and machine interpretation.

Returning to the mirror motif, bias distorts because models reflect statistical histories, not moral expectations. Histories contain power imbalances. Models reproduce them until someone draws a line. But drawing the line is only the start. Organisations must commit to periodic audits. Brookhaven now runs quarterly counterfactual tests on a random 10 percent of screened résumés. Riverside Finance audits postcode dispersion every month. The Edinburgh triage team reviews false negatives weekly. Oversight becomes habitual when embedded in cadence rather than triggered by scandal.

But bias tests alone are insufficient. Human judgement must accompany detection. A machine may flag disparities; only people can decide whether the disparity is reasonable. For example, an apprenticeship programme in Birmingham noticed that older applicants were passing their automated assessments at lower rates. An initial hypothesis pointed to age bias. But deeper analysis, conducted in March 2023, revealed a different driver: the assessments relied on tasks that assumed familiarity with specific software used mainly in schools and universities in the last five years. The behaviour—struggling with interface-specific tasks—was a skills issue, not a demographic prejudice. The counter-example reinforces a critical truth: not every disparity is bias, and not every bias is visible. Oversight requires emotional humility as well as analytical precision.

The broader implication emerges here: organisations need internal cultures that treat bias detection as a routine act of stewardship, not an accusation. When the Brookhaven team discovered the CV disparity, their reaction was neither shame nor defensiveness. It was curiosity followed by responsibility. They fixed the dataset, reran the model, and revised their deployment protocol. Their behaviour communicated a simple principle: oversight is not an admission of failure but a sign of care.

This principle leads us to the next point: fairness demands transparency. Transparent criteria. Transparent data lineage. Transparent thresholds. When candidates, employees, or customers understand how systems operate, trust becomes more stable. Trust is a behaviour—a willingness to interact, comply, or continue. And trust deteriorates when people sense that decisions are made in obscure ways. Transparency is therefore not a courtesy but a safeguard.

But transparency has limits too. Organisations cannot always reveal every parameter of a commercial model. They cannot expose sensitive security thresholds. The limitation is real. Reconciliation lies in distinguishing between revealing *logic* and revealing *implementation*. Brookhaven published the rationale behind its screening criteria without releasing proprietary weights. Riverside explained that postcode-based correlations were reviewed but not directly used. The Edinburgh triage team briefed patients on how tools supported—not replaced—nurse judgement. The pattern holds: transparency about intent stabilises trust even when complete disclosure is impossible.

Now the mirror motif returns one last time. Every algorithm reflects the structure of its training data, but oversight reflects the moral choices of those who deploy it. The mirror can show cracks or clarity. What teams do with the reflection determines whether the tool serves or harms.

The unresolved tension surfaces as a final prompt: what happens when bias is suspected but not yet measurable? Should deployment pause? Should teams gather more evidence? Should they adjust workflows or redesign features? There is no universal rule. But the forward test remains constant. Ask yourself: if the system is wrong, who is harmed, and how quickly? The answer determines the urgency of oversight—and whether the mirror must be cleaned before the system can run again.

Privacy by design

At 07:58 on 14 February 2023, the intake nurse at Calder Medical Centre in Huddersfield opened the revised patient registration form that had gone live that morning. The redesign, finalised the previous week, cut the form from thirty-two fields to fourteen. No employment details. No household income. No unnecessary contact notes. The clinic's director, Dr Anna Hart, had argued forcefully in January that most of these fields were artefacts of habit, not care. What mattered were symptoms, medications, allergies, and a reliable way to reach the patient. Everything else created drag and risk. By April, the centre had recorded a measurable shift: a 17 percent reduction in form-completion time (internal audit, Calder Medical Centre, 2023) and a fall in failed follow-ups because staff could locate essential data faster. The clinic had encrypted all fields by default and implemented role-based access that segmented who could see what. Yet service quality rose. Privacy did not slow care; it sharpened it.

The scene illustrates a principle that sits at the centre of this subchapter—the container. Privacy by design is not about making systems opaque; it is about shaping the container that holds personal information so tightly and deliberately that nothing spills unnecessarily. Intelligent systems invite organisations to gather more: more data, more context, more inputs, more behavioural traces. The temptation is understandable. More data promises smoother prediction. But data is weight. Data is liability. And data, when stored without discipline, becomes a quiet threat to the very people it is meant to serve.

To see how design choices shape outcomes, begin with behaviour, not abstraction. At Calder, staff no longer asked about employment because they realised it had never once changed a clinical decision. Name the underlying principle: data minimisation. Explain: collect only what is required to achieve a specific, clearly stated purpose. Implication: when an organisation reduces data intake, two things happen simultaneously—risk shrinks and clarity grows. Clinicians spend less time filtering noise. Systems process fewer irrelevant fields. Patients sense respect.

A second named example broadens the frame. In September 2022, the South London Therapy Partnership introduced a new consent process for its telehealth platform. The platform previously captured call metadata—locations, durations, device details—without presenting clients with meaningful choice. Complaints rose, especially from those in precarious housing situations who feared their data might reach landlords or insurers. The Partnership rewrote its consent pattern over two weeks. Now clients see exactly which data fields are collected, why they are collected, and how long they are stored. Calls are encrypted end-to-end, and metadata is minimised. Six months later, attendance rates increased by 11 percent (Partnership Operational Review, March 2023). The behaviour is telling: when people understand and trust data practices, they participate more freely.

Yet privacy by design is not frictionless. A counter-example reveals a limitation. In 2021, a Midlands-based physiotherapy chain attempted to anonymise patient data for internal research. They removed names, dates of birth, and postcodes, assuming this was enough. It wasn't. Re-identification became possible through unique combinations of injury type and appointment timestamps. When the issue surfaced during a data-protection review in 2022, the chain suspended its analytics until it could implement true pseudonymisation. The limitation teaches a blunt truth: minimisation is not only about collecting less; it is about designing systems that cannot be reverse-engineered. Reconciliation lies in adopting layered privacy—strip identifiers, reduce granularity, segment access, and monitor re-identification attempts.

Returning to the container motif, consider why intelligent systems make privacy discipline both more urgent and more complex. Every model has an appetite. It pulls data inward to generate predictions. But not all inputs contribute meaningfully. At Calder, Dr Hart noticed the intake form included a field for "preferred pharmacy", but the clinic already used an electronic prescription system that automatically identified the nearest option. Removing the field did not reduce capability; it removed redundancy. That behaviour—interrogating each field—became part of the clinic's routine. Name the habit: purpose alignment. Explain: map every data point to a decision. If no decision depends on it, it has no justification for remaining inside the container. Implication: staff become guardians, not gatherers.

The privacy container also depends on technical infrastructure. Encryption at rest and in transit sounds obvious, but its implications are profound. At Calder, all data flows—form submission, laboratory results, referral requests—were encrypted by default. This meant that even internal e-mails carrying attachments were replaced with secure links. The visible behaviour was a drop in accidental data exposure incidents, from five in 2022 to zero in the first half of 2023. Encryption alone did not create trust, but it reduced the surface area of harm.

Role-based access built the next layer. Calder restricted who could view certain fields. Reception staff saw contact details and appointment histories. Clinicians saw symptoms and treatment notes. Administrators saw only aggregated usage data. The behaviour that mattered was simple: when staff clicked into a record, irrelevant fields were absent. That absence is powerful. It prevents temptation, reduces error, and signals respect. Name the principle: least privilege. Explain: nobody should access more than they need to fulfil their role. Implication: if a breach happens, the blast radius shrinks dramatically.

Privacy by design also means designing spaces for consent. Many organisations treat consent as a compliance requirement rather than a relational act. But consent is behaviour: reading, understanding, agreeing—or refusing. In the South London case, rewriting consent transformed it from a legal checkbox into a conversation. Clients were shown practical examples of what the platform did and did not store. They were told how to withdraw consent and what that withdrawal would affect. The transparency changed participation. Anxiety lowered. The container felt safer.

The pattern holds in other sectors. Consider an educational technology company in Oxford that deployed a classroom feedback tool in October 2022. Initially, it captured detailed keystroke logs to detect student engagement. Parents protested. Teachers resisted. The company pivoted. They reduced data granularity, capturing only event markers (submission time, completion status, help-request flags). They anonymised logs for analytics. They added a dashboard that allowed parents to see exactly what was recorded. A year later, adoption increased across eighteen schools. Here, the behaviour was ownership: giving stakeholders visibility into the container's walls.

A limitation arises, however, when organisations collect too little. Minimisation can overshoot. A community health project in Bristol attempted to strip its intake form down to six fields. But without basic demographic data, the team struggled to monitor disparities in service quality. They reinstated a small set of fields that genuinely mattered. The lesson: minimisation must be paired with measurement. Collect enough to ensure equity and safety, but no more.

Privacy by design therefore becomes an exercise in tension: gather enough information to serve people well, but not so much that the container becomes bloated or porous. The motif strengthens here: the container must be proportionate to its contents. Overfill it, and it becomes unstable. Underfill it, and it loses function.

Where does machine intelligence fit? In Calder's case, introducing an AI-supported triage assistant did not require new fields. It required cleaner ones. The model performed better because it processed fewer, more reliable inputs. That behaviour—improved accuracy through less data—contradicts the common assumption that privacy constrains quality. Sometimes it does the opposite.

Oversight remains crucial. Privacy by design is not a single act but a recurring posture. Calder now runs quarterly "field justification reviews" where each data point must earn its place. South London reviews consent patterns every six months. The Oxford ed-tech firm publishes a data-transparency report each quarter. These rhythms make privacy visible rather than implicit.

Yet unresolved tensions remain. When a service improves through minimised data today, what prevents someone from expanding the container tomorrow? How do teams ensure that minimisation sticks when new tools arrive, new leaders take over, or new ambitions tempt them to gather more? And what happens when a model appears to perform better with richer data—should privacy bend, or should capability?

These questions sit at the edge of responsible design. The test is simple but demanding: if you removed half the data your system currently collects, which decisions would genuinely suffer—and which would simply feel less convenient? Privacy by design begins where that question stops being avoided and starts being answered.

Safety cases and boundaries

At 06:42 on 11 May 2022, the operations lead at SkyPath Logistics, a drone-delivery start-up based in Swindon, watched a test flight freeze mid-route. The quadcopter had reached the western boundary of a hard-coded no-fly zone mapped to the Great Western Hospital. Instead of correcting course on its own, it halted, descended to a safe altitude, and returned along its inbound trajectory. Engineers later confirmed that the geofence had prevented the drone straying into medical airspace where emergency helicopters landed routinely. The incident was uneventful, almost boring, and that was the point. The safety case drafted three months earlier had insisted on visible, testable boundaries before any system scaled. By July, SkyPath secured clearance for a larger pilot programme because its operating envelope—normal conditions, abnormal conditions, and red-line prohibitions—was already defined and demonstrated.

The scene captures a recurring truth: the most sophisticated intelligent systems depend on something deceptively simple—agreements about what they must never do. Without those agreements, complexity turns brittle. With them, complexity gains structure. Every safety case, no matter how technical, begins with a line in the sand.

To understand why boundaries matter, begin with behaviour rather than principle. At SkyPath, the no-fly zone forced the drone to *stop*, not improvise. Name the idea: operating envelope. Explain: a model or machine performs only within a specified range of acceptable behaviours, and any deviation triggers a safe response. Implication: reliability becomes observable. Instead of trusting intention, regulators and operators trust patterns of action.

A second example shows the same logic in a different domain. In November 2020, Transport for London approved a limited deployment of autonomous street-cleaning units in the City. The approval depended on a tightly defined safety case that limited operation to early-morning windows, low-footfall streets, and capped speeds of 4 mph. The units carried an edge-based vision system and a failsafe that forced them to brake when sensing ambiguous motion within two metres. Within six months, the pilot expanded. The behaviour that persuaded officials was not the units' accuracy; it was their predictability. The machines obeyed their envelope.

Yet safety cases can fail when envelopes are poorly drawn. A counter-example from industrial robotics illustrates the limitation. In 2019, a Midlands manufacturing plant introduced a collaborative robot meant to assist with part assembly. Its operating envelope assumed workers would stay outside a marked zone during automated cycles. But the envelope ignored real human behaviour: staff often leaned in to adjust components while the robot idled between tasks. In March 2020, a near-miss occurred when the machine restarted as an operator reached across the boundary. Investigators found that the safety case focused on the robot's performance, not workers' habits. The envelope was redesigned to include presence detection and speed-and-separation monitoring. Reconciliation came from expanding the definition of "normal" human activity—not forcing workers into unrealistic discipline.

This interplay—between what a system can do and what people *actually* do—threads through all responsible design. Boundaries must reflect lived behaviour, not imagined order. That is why the safety case is best viewed through a quiet motif: the map. A good safety case is a map of where a system is allowed to go, what terrains are forbidden, and where emergency routes lie. A map does not remove uncertainty; it channels it.

To translate a safety case into everyday decisions, begin with what users see. At SkyPath, pilots and operators received a one-page checklist. It listed three things: pre-flight environment checks, boundary verification, and failsafe status. The visible behaviour was routine: before each launch, an operator confirmed that the boundaries loaded correctly. Name the practice: pre-condition testing. Explain: the system should only operate when the world around it matches its assumptions. Implication: anomalies are caught early, not when a drone hovers over protected airspace.

A second behaviour anchors the map motif. SkyPath colour-coded its operating envelope: green for conditions where drones could act autonomously; amber for conditions that required operator supervision; red for conditions where drones must not fly. Operators could see these zones on their tablet interface. The map was literal. The clarity mattered. Ambiguity is where accidents hide.

Another checkable example expands the scope. In August 2021, the Norwegian Maritime Authority approved the Yara Birkeland, an autonomous electric cargo vessel, for limited service between Herøya and Brevik. Its safety case delineated clear rules: the vessel must hand off control to a human operator when encountering dense fog or irregular shipping traffic; must maintain specific standoff distances; and must follow fixed geofenced lanes. These boundaries allowed regulators to approve a world-first autonomous container ship because they could see the map, test it, and understand its edges. The implication is profound:

autonomy scales not through boldness but through constraint.

Yet constraints can be politically and operationally painful. A credible limitation emerges from emergency services. In 2022, a European fire-rescue consortium tested AI-assisted triage drones for large-scale incidents. Early prototypes adhered to strict operating envelopes that disallowed flying over active fire lines or within ten metres of ground crews. Commanders criticised the restrictions as too conservative; drones missed opportunities to capture useful data. Adjusting the envelope required negotiation between safety experts, engineers, and frontline teams. The reconciliation came from redesigning failsafes—thermal sensors, manual override triggers, and operator-in-the-loop pauses—that allowed the envelope to widen without eroding trust. The lesson: an envelope must adapt, but never at the expense of clarity.

Safety cases also hinge on failure modes. The map must include escape routes. At SkyPath, every drone included a "return-to-base" protocol triggered by signal loss, battery anomalies, or boundary violations. Operators practised these triggers weekly. The behaviour mattered: humans rehearsed what failure looked like. The system was not trusted to improvise. Name the concept: failsafe choreography. Explain: in safety-critical settings, recovery behaviour must be as predictable as normal behaviour. Implication: emergencies become manageable, not catastrophic.

Notice how the map motif returns. Every safety case is a map with two layers: the route and the exit. Organisations that scale responsibly draw both.

But safety cases are more than technical artefacts. They are social compacts. They define acceptable risk, articulate shared responsibility, and set expectations for escalation. In Swindon, SkyPath maintained an internal escalation path: if a drone breached a boundary—even hypothetically during simulation—engineers paused deployments until they could trace and explain the breach. That behaviour built confidence among local authorities. A map gains authority when it is updated honestly, not silently.

Other organisations have learned this the hard way. In 2020, a German warehouse deployed an AI-based forklift navigation system. Its safety case assumed the forklifts would follow predetermined paths. But when pallets accumulated unpredictably, operators rerouted forklifts manually, drifting beyond the assumed envelope. When a near collision occurred in December, investigators discovered that the safety case had never been translated into daily checklist form. It lived as a PDF, not a practice. The limitation teaches something essential: a safety case dies when it becomes static text.

This is why translation matters. A good safety case moves from document to ritual. SkyPath operators use their checklist before every shift. Yara Birkeland's navigation team reviews envelope deviations weekly. Fire-rescue drone pilots rehearse override drills monthly. The map must be walked repeatedly.

The broader implication for intelligent systems is clear: boundaries are not obstacles to progress; they are what allow progress to endure. Without them, every system drifts into untested terrain. With them, systems earn permission to scale.

Yet unresolved questions remain. As models grow more capable, should envelopes shrink or expand? When a system learns to identify new edge cases, what stops an organisation from moving the red lines outward without adequate scrutiny? And at what point does a safety case become a shield—protecting people—or a crutch—limiting necessary evolution?

The forward test is blunt. If you widened your system's operating envelope tomorrow, could you justify that expansion with behaviour, data, and transparent oversight? Or would the map grow simply because the technology feels ready, even if the organisation is not?

Safety cases and boundaries exist to prevent that drift. They force the discipline of proof over intuition. They tell a system where it may go, but more importantly, where it must never step.

Dignity at work

At 08:17 on 3 March 2021, the operations floor of Meridian Contact Solutions in Sheffield paused for an announcement.

A new performance-scoring system—introduced the previous autumn—had been criticised by staff for producing opaque ratings. After weeks of tension, the company published the full scoring logic on an internal dashboard: weightings for call resolution, hold-time behaviour, customer sentiment scores derived from a natural language model, and penalties for repeated transfers. More strikingly, the dashboard included an appeal button. When agents challenged their scores, supervisors had to review the call transcripts, the model's confidence metrics, and any contextual notes. Within three months, Meridian reported a measurable outcome: appeal volumes fell, not because the system became less strict, but because workers finally understood the rules. An efficiency tool had ceased to be a hidden judge.

The episode captures a deeper claim. People can accept discipline when its contours are visible; they resist when the machine feels capricious. Efficiency without clarity corrodes dignity. Efficiency with clarity can support it. The question is not whether organisations should measure work, but how they should behave towards the people whose labour those measurements represent.

Dignity begins with recognition. Show it, name it, explain it. When Meridian published its scoring logic, it acknowledged workers as partners rather than subjects. Name the principle: explainability. Explain: people deserve to know how they are being assessed, especially when automated systems influence pay, progression, or retention.

Implication: trust becomes observable. We see it when a supervisor sits with an agent to unpack the sentiment model's reasoning, or when an appeal leads to a corrected score and a revised weighting.

The motif that threads through this account is *the window*. Systems that preserve dignity install windows—transparent openings through which workers can see the structure that evaluates them. Opaque walls signal hierarchy. Windows signal mutual respect.

Consider a second example, drawn from healthcare. In January 2020, the National Health Service Highland region introduced an AI-supported triage system for outpatient referrals. The system recommended risk categories, but clinicians retained authority over final classification. Importantly, nurses and administrators could view the model's variables, see its risk thresholds, and annotate exceptions. This visibility mattered when, in August that year, staff identified a pattern: women in rural clinics were disproportionately flagged as low-risk, likely due to data gaps from inconsistent recording in earlier years. Because the window existed, the bias was spotted quickly. The system was retrained. The implication is clear: explainability is not a courtesy feature; it is the mechanism through which dignity and accuracy reinforce one another.

Yet windows can mislead when they show only partial truth. A counter-example emerged in 2022 at a European retail bank that deployed an AI to monitor call-centre compliance. The system displayed a dashboard of behavioural flags—speaking pace, silence durations, and instances of regulatory language—but these were only proxies for what managers actually judged. Staff believed the dashboard governed performance, not realising that supervisors relied more heavily on call recordings. The limitation here is stark: transparency becomes theatre when the window shows a simplified shadow of the real evaluative process. Reconciliation requires coherence. A window must show what truly matters, not what is easiest to display.

If explainability is the first norm, the second is consent—real, operational consent. In 2021, a Dublin-based insurer introduced an opt-out for call analytics. Agents could request exclusion from automated scoring for a defined period, usually during training, recovery from illness, or personal stress. Managers initially feared reduced oversight. Instead, the metric that changed most was attrition: staff turnover fell by 12% over nine months (company report, 2022). Workers opted back in once they felt confident again. The behaviour shows a principle: autonomy supports retention. Name it: bounded opt-out. Explain: workers can decline algorithmic evaluation without forfeiting trust or opportunity. Implication: dignity becomes a design choice, not a by-product.

This brings the window motif back into view. Opt-outs widen the window. They show that the system sees workers as people with rhythms, limits, and seasons—not as constant data emitters.

A third norm concerns rest. In early 2023, a study by the UK Health and Safety Executive (HSE) highlighted that contact-centre employees working under automated measurement regimes experienced higher micro-fatigue episodes—brief lapses in attention—compared to those under human-only evaluation (HSE, 2023). Fatigue metrics appeared in the study: increased silence intervals and elevated error rates during post-lunch shifts. The response from one company, Northshore Utilities in Sunderland, was practical. They inserted protected recovery intervals—unmeasured breaks between blocks of high-intensity calls. These were scheduled, visible, and non-negotiable. The behaviour changed: agents slowed their speech less in the final hour of each shift. Managers reported fewer flagged compliance deviations. Rest restored quality.

The implication is firm. Efficiency that consumes rest consumes reliability. Systems that honour rest cycles preserve dignity precisely because they acknowledge human physiology. A body is not an algorithm, and a humane workplace does not pretend otherwise.

This framework—windows of transparency, moments of consent, and spaces of rest—turns abstract dignity into visible action. Yet dignity is not only about conditions; it is about narrative. People seek coherence in how they are treated. When a system evaluates someone silently, it erodes their sense of authorship. When a system explains itself, invites response, and respects limits, it restores that authorship.

One more example illustrates how narrative, transparency, and agency coalesce. In 2022, the city of Rotterdam partnered with researchers to trial an AI-supported scheduling system for public works crews. The model aimed to balance workload, travel distance, and skill distribution. Workers initially feared micromanagement. The project leaders responded with a design change: they held weekly briefings where crews reviewed the system's outputs, challenged anomalies, and co-authored updates to the scheduling rules. This co-authorship had an outcome: scheduling accuracy improved, and team satisfaction scores rose (Municipal Report, December 2022). The dignity came not from soft gestures but from structural inclusion.

Yet not every attempt succeeds. In 2020, a warehouse operator in the Midlands deployed wearable sensors that tracked worker movement to optimise shift allocation. The sensors displayed real-time "utilisation scores" on a dashboard visible to supervisors. Although the company published its scoring logic, it offered no opt-outs and no rest protections. Workers reported increased stress and a sense of being surveilled. In February 2021, after a public inquiry, the programme was suspended. The limitation lies in the asymmetry: transparency without agency can heighten anxiety rather than reduce it. The window opened, but the workers remained locked behind it.

Reconciliation comes from aligning three elements: transparency, agency, and boundary. A system respects dignity when these three align. If one is missing, the design falters. If two are missing, dignity collapses.

The question that organisations must ask—quietly but relentlessly—is this: what does our system assume about the people who work within it? The assumptions surface in the smallest details. Does the interface presume unlimited attention? Does the scoring logic presume uniform context? Does the escalation path presume silent acceptance? Every assumption is a bet about human nature. Some bets honour workers; others instrumentalise them.

This is why dignity cannot be added as an afterthought. It must appear in the design brief. It must shape the boundaries of data collection, the cadence of feedback, and the flow of appeals. It must be drawn into the architecture of tools before those tools reach production.

The window motif returns once more. A dignified workplace is one where people can see into the system that shapes their experience—and see themselves reflected in its logic. They do not see a distant, indifferent machine; they see norms, compromises, and guardrails that acknowledge their humanity.

But an unresolved tension remains. How far should transparency go before it compromises security, proprietary logic, or performance? When does opting out become an operational risk? And how should organisations reconcile collective fairness with individual preference?

The forward test is simple to ask and difficult to meet: if every employee saw the system that evaluates them—its inputs, assumptions, and consequences—would they recognise themselves in it? Or would they feel managed by a stranger?

In that answer lies the line between efficiency and dignity.

Chapter 6
Education That Fits the Future

On a grey Tuesday morning in October 2022, a group of twelve-year-olds at a public school in Wellington gathered for what their timetable still called "Science," though the class barely resembled the subject their parents remembered. The room held no rows of desks, no timed worksheets, no frantic memorisation before a test. Instead, the pupils stood in a semicircle around a prototype water-filter they had been trying to improve for weeks. One team argued that their charcoal layer absorbed too slowly; another suggested rewriting the criteria altogether because the original brief—"clean water"—was far too vague. Their teacher, instead of announcing answers, pressed them with questions: Which assumption is weakest? What evidence would change your mind? Who might use this device, and under what constraints? The project would end not with a written exam but with a critique studio, where students defended their reasoning to peers. Knowledge was present, certainly, but it was no longer the star. What mattered was judgement—how these young people framed problems, worked with uncertainty, and justified decisions.

That small classroom captured something the wider education system has been struggling to articulate: the institutions designed to sort people by how well they recall facts are ill-suited to a world where facts are everywhere, instantly accessible, and often generated by machines. What remains scarce is the human capacity to interrogate, interpret, and apply. The tension is simple to state yet transformative in consequence. We know more than ever; we understand no better by default. And so the value of education shifts: away from the mere possession of information and towards the disciplined habits that make information mean something.

For more than a century, mass education treated learning as accumulation. Its architects built factories of cognition: highly regulated, time-bound, standardised. Workers for an industrial economy needed predictable knowledge executed at predictable speed. Today, that formula buckles under the weight of automation. A child can access more data in a few keystrokes than a university library once held on entire shelves. Software drafts essays, solves equations, and offers plausible explanations before students even begin to wrestle with the material. Yet the need for educators has not diminished. It has sharpened. Machines can generate outputs; they cannot reliably cultivate discernment. They can model patterns; they cannot teach what counts, or why.

We stand at a moment where the institution most responsible for shaping citizens confronts a paradox: intelligence has been outsourced, but wisdom has not. Whether we treat this as crisis or opportunity depends on how boldly we rethink the foundations.

This chapter examines how education must evolve—not through flashy digitisation or the naïve worship of novelty, but through a deeper reconstruction of purpose. It begins with the recognition that judgement is not an optional layer sprinkled atop curriculum maps; it is the organising principle of modern learning. A school in Helsinki that replaced rote science exams with critique studios did so not as an experiment in progressive pedagogy, but as an acknowledgment that students who can deconstruct arguments and surface assumptions are better prepared for any discipline than students who can merely recite definitions. The shift is subtle but decisive: the centre of gravity moves from what students know to how they think.

From there, the chapter turns to assessment—not as punishment or credential, but as a public demonstration of reasoning. When a university in Glasgow piloted viva-style finals for computer science students in 2023, the faculty were responding to a practical challenge: how to evaluate originality when AI tools can produce code that looks sophisticated yet lacks conceptual depth. The oral defence forced students to articulate choices, justify deviations, and situate their work within broader contexts. Cheating, once a matter of spotting copied text, now required interrogating the coherence of someone's thought. Assessment regained its role as a mirror rather than a gate.

This reorientation extends beyond academic settings. Trades, often romanticised as untouched by automation, find themselves leading the next educational transformation. Skilled manual work has always demanded a fusion of tacit knowledge, sensory acuity, and situational awareness—attributes machines struggle to emulate. Yet robotics and augmented reality now enhance, rather than diminish, this embodied intelligence. An electrician in Birmingham who uses an AR checklist to reduce wiring errors is not replacing craft with gadgetry; he is freeing cognitive space to teach apprentices why certain decisions matter. The craft survives not because it resists technology, but because it integrates it responsibly.

The motif that threads through all these domains is continuity. Education cannot be conceived as a finite stage that ends with graduation. A life is longer than any curriculum, and the skills that matter—interpretation, collaboration, ethical judgement—demand renewal. The infrastructure of lifelong learning, still embryonic, must mature. A community college in Portland provides a glimpse of direction: issuing skill passports that record not just courses completed but projects produced, peer reviews, reflections, and problem-solving episodes. Local employers use these passports as signals of capability, not mere compliance. The learner becomes legible not through a transcript but through a narrative of practice.

This shift raises deeper questions. Who owns the learner's history? What counts as evidence of growth? And how should schools, universities, and workplaces share responsibility for nurturing people whose working lives may span half a dozen professions and technologies not yet conceived? These are not administrative puzzles. They are structural challenges that force us to reconsider education as a system of shared stewardship rather than a narrow pipeline.

What emerges, then, is a picture of education that is less about delivery and more about coherence: coherence between what we teach and the world students encounter; coherence between the skills we reward and the values we claim to uphold; coherence between the rapid evolution of technology and the slower evolution of human judgement. We can no longer afford a model where students learn alone, teachers teach alone, and workers reskill alone. The future demands distributed responsibility.

And so this chapter invites the reader to consider three intertwined propositions. First, that human judgement, not factual recall, is the scarce resource around which curricula must be rebuilt. Second, that assessment must become a transparent exploration of thinking, not a ritual of sorting. Third, that education's purpose is not to prepare people for a single career, but to equip them with the habits necessary to navigate many: curiosity, resilience, ethical imagination, and the capacity to learn in public.

Yet an unresolved tension shadows this transformation. If we ask institutions to teach what machines cannot, are we willing to redesign those institutions from the ground up? If we replace exams with studios, transcripts with portfolios, and fixed curricula with evolving maps of competence, what becomes of the systems—bureaucratic, cultural, political—that rely on old forms of certainty?

These questions do not weaken the case for change. They sharpen it. And they leave us facing a quiet test: when the future arrives in the form of a new tool, a new expectation, or a new uncertainty, will our educational structures expand to meet it—or collapse under the weight of their own inertia?

That question, more than any syllabus or standard, will determine whether education fits the future, or forces the future to fit an outdated idea of education.

Curricula for judgement

In September 2019, at Te Kura o Ōtaki on New Zealand's Kapiti Coast, a group of Year 10 pupils filed into a converted art room expecting, as usual, the pressure of a timed science test. Instead, their teacher, Maia Rangi, handed out a single sheet with no questions and no marks. At the top of the page was a short description of a stormwater problem affecting a nearby marae: pooling after heavy rain, contamination after runoff, and the rising cost of manual drainage. "Your task," she told them, "is to decide what the real problem is." The pupils argued for forty minutes. Some framed the issue as engineering, others as ecology, one as a budgeting constraint, another as a cultural stewardship duty. The assessment ended not with a score but with a critique studio, where classmates challenged each team's assumptions. That afternoon, Rangi recorded the highest engagement levels her school had seen in the term. Not because the pupils knew more science, but because they were finally being asked to use what they knew to make sense of a messy, situated question.

The scene captured a shift too many systems acknowledge but have not yet enacted: the migration of value from knowing to framing. Facts remain indispensable, but they no longer differentiate. What distinguishes one learner from another—indeed, one professional from another—is the ability to interrogate context, clarify purpose, and surface the constraints that shape any meaningful decision. A curriculum centred on judgement does not diminish knowledge; it arranges knowledge in service of something more durable.

The modern classroom still mirrors its industrial ancestors in one crucial respect: it privileges recall. The model has persisted for pragmatic reasons. Recall is cheap to test, easy to standardise, and politically comfortable. But as early as the 1980s, education researchers like Lauren Resnick argued that genuine intellectual competence involves "reasoning under uncertainty," something traditional exams rarely probe. The contest today is no longer between progressive and traditional pedagogues; it is between those who continue to teach memorisation as a proxy for thinking and those who recognise that students will live and work alongside systems that can summon information far faster than they can.

The shift from facts to framing demands new modules, not decorative add-ons but structural reconfigurations. Consider problem definition, a skill often treated as tacit. In

Rangi's classroom, pupils were forced to articulate competing interpretations: Is the stormwater issue fundamentally about hydraulics, environmental impact, or cultural safeguarding? Each framing produced different solution paths. Teaching problem definition explicitly—through comparative cases, reflective prompts, and dispute analysis—turns a passive learner into an intentional one. When a cohort at the University of Melbourne piloted a problem-framing module in 2020, students who previously spent minutes skimming a prompt now spent half their time clarifying what the prompt should have been. The module did not make them more knowledgeable; it made them more responsible for their own reasoning.

Ethics follows naturally. A curriculum for judgement cannot treat ethics as a narrow domain reserved for philosophers. It must be the connective tissue that binds scientific, technical, and social decisions. The Ōtaki case was instructive: some pupils insisted that any solution must preserve the mana of the marae, regardless of cost. Others prioritised water quality metrics. The tension became a living classroom, revealing something the pupils would later see in broader civic life: that ethical principles and empirical data sit in constant negotiation. When schools in Oslo introduced structured ethical deliberations into their technology courses in 2021, they discovered that pupils became more sceptical of "optimising" solutions that ignored social consequences. Ethics, taught this way, is not moralising; it is a disciplined habit of anticipating externalities.

Experimentation forms the third pillar. The capacity to test, observe, and revise is foundational not only to science but to any field that confronts uncertainty. Yet schools often reduce experimentation to cookbook labs: pre-defined, linear, and insulated from failure. A curriculum for judgement must do the opposite. It must foreground the open-ended. In Singapore, the Ministry of Education's Applied Learning Programme (ALP) has, since 2013, encouraged pupils to run multi-week investigations with poorly specified outcomes. Teachers report that the hardest part is not managing unpredictability but resisting the urge to rescue students from it. The pupils who flourish learn to articulate hypotheses, defend them provisionally, and abandon them gracefully when evidence shifts. That disposition—tentative confidence paired with methodological humility—is the engine of judgement.

These three modules—problem definition, ethics, experimentation—share a quiet motif: friction. They introduce cognitive resistance that timed recall tests systematically avoid. Yet friction is precisely the point. It slows thinking enough for learners to notice their assumptions. It gives teachers a lens onto the reasoning process rather than its results.

Building such modules, however, requires abandoning a longstanding myth: that judgement is innate. Systems that reward only correct answers reinforce the belief that capacity is fixed. In contrast, critique studios like Rangi's make reasoning public and improvable. Pupils learn to welcome scrutiny, not fear it. They see that framing is a craft—and like any craft, it can be taught, practised, and refined. The studios also reveal a pragmatic truth: most students are far more capable of conceptual debate than traditional curricula allow. They rise to the challenge when the challenge feels real.

Examples from other contexts underscore the point. In 2020, a history teacher at King Edward VI School in Birmingham replaced a final exam with a source-framing exercise. Students were given four primary documents about the same event—the 1936 Jarrow March—and asked to argue not what happened, but what each source *assumed* had happened. The work was strong enough that two pupils later submitted their analyses to the Historical Association's national competition. Meanwhile, in Kyoto, a secondary school introduced a cross-disciplinary module where students framed climate-related dilemmas faced by local businesses. Here, the teachers found something counter-intuitive: the students who excelled were not those with the highest test scores but those who habitually asked clarifying questions.

There are limitations. Not every teacher is trained in facilitation; not every school can redesign assessments without bureaucratic pushback; and not every student initially enjoys the uncertainty these modules create. But these criticisms do not undermine the approach. They illuminate where support must grow. Curriculum reform that centres judgement demands investment in teacher development, flexible timetables, and evaluation systems that reward thoughtful risk.

The shift also invites uncomfortable questions about equity. If judgement is increasingly valued, will students from more privileged backgrounds—who already receive conversational, debate-rich stimulation at home—pull further ahead? Evidence from a 2018 study by the Education Endowment Foundation suggests the opposite: structured reasoning activities reduce gaps by making implicit reasoning explicit. Pupils from all backgrounds benefit when teachers model how to question premises, track evidence, and articulate uncertainty. The advantage shifts from cultural familiarity to disciplined method.

Throughout this chapter, one motif recurs: peeling back. Good judgement begins with peeling back the surface of a task, revealing the structure beneath. It applies to sorting stormwater problems; it applies to interpreting historical documents; it applies to navigating moral tension. A curriculum that cultivates this ability equips students not simply to answer questions, but to discover which questions deserve attention.

Assessment must then change accordingly. In 2022, a school in Dublin replaced traditional end-of-year exams in its Transition Year with studio-style critiques similar to those in design schools. Students presented their reasoning processes in front of panels including teachers, peers, and local community members. The panels assessed clarity, rigour, and adaptability, not memorised content. One teacher noted that previously quiet pupils became articulate defenders of their own thinking. Meanwhile, high-achieving pupils struggled when forced to justify methods rather than recall information. The exercise was revelatory because it made visible what conventional tests obscure: that judgement is unevenly distributed but highly trainable.

But the reform prompts an unresolved tension. As universities and employers continue to rely on grades as signals, can schools afford to abandon traditional exams? Or is this precisely the moment they must lead, forcing downstream institutions to adjust? The question is not trivial. It touches on political risk, parental expectations, and the lingering belief that certainty in measurement is synonymous with rigour.

The tension invites a deeper consideration: if curricula pivot to judgement, what must be sacrificed? Some content will inevitably be displaced. The reflexive objection—that without extensive coverage students will lack foundational knowledge—misses a structural point. The foundation is not breadth of recall but the ability to construct meaning from information regardless of how it is delivered. Knowledge still matters, but as material rather than master. A student adept in framing, ethics, and experimentation will learn facts quickly when needed; a student who merely memorises facts will struggle to frame new problems when old ones fade.

At the core of this transformation lies an ethical commitment. To teach judgement is to trust students with complexity. It is an act of respect: acknowledging that they can handle ambiguity and debate. Systems that limit them to recall betray a quieter cynicism: the assumption that young people cannot be trusted with thinking that may challenge authority or disrupt tidy answers.

As educational technologies proliferate—automated marking, personalised learning dashboards, generative assistants—the temptation will be to automate reasoning as well as recall. But the future of education rests not on delegating thinking to machines but on preparing human beings to think well alongside machines. Curricula for judgement do precisely that. They ensure that tools become catalysts, not crutches.

And so the chapter ends with a question every institution must now confront: if students graduate knowing many things but unable to frame a single unfamiliar problem with clarity and conscience, have we educated them at all?

Assessment in an AI age

In May 2023, the University of Edinburgh ran an experiment that unsettled its own assumptions about examination. Instead of the usual three-hour written paper for its second-year political theory course, it piloted viva-style finals in a seminar room overlooking George Square. Students submitted a short written brief two days earlier. Their grade, however, depended chiefly on a fifteen-minute oral defence before two assessors. One candidate, unsure yet composed, began by outlining how her argument had shifted after a counterexample raised in her study group. Another showed the evolution of his reasoning by opening a notebook filled with crossed-out premises and revised hypotheses. When the results were released in June, examiners noted a rare convergence: the strongest performances were not the most polished briefs, but the clearest displays of thinking. The university's internal review recorded a drop in suspected misconduct cases for the module—from six the previous year to none. The intervention did not make cheating impossible; it made authenticity more visible.

The pilots revealed what many institutions have been slow to recognise: when generative tools can draft fluent text within seconds, fluency ceases to be evidence of understanding. If assessment is to remain meaningful, it must detect what machines cannot convincingly imitate at scale—reasoning steps, collaborative judgement, and contextual originality. The shift is not cosmetic; it changes the very substrate of what counts as evidence. And once evidence changes, the design of every assessment must follow.

The problem is structural. Traditional assessments capture outputs, not processes. A timed essay reduces thinking to product; a multiple-choice test compresses complexity into recognition; even coursework essays, long treated as the gold standard of intellectual effort, now risk becoming artefacts that obscure more reasoning than they reveal. The Edinburgh pilot surfaced a small but essential truth: when students narrate how they reached a claim, the examiner gains insight that no static script can provide. Oral defences compel students to show their working. They slow the rush to polish. They make reasoning accountable.

The principle has precedent. In 1998, the University of Oxford introduced compulsory viva voce examinations in several humanities departments to verify borderline cases and suspected anomalies. Though modest in scale, the shift acknowledged something the classical tradition understood intuitively: argument is a living act. But the contemporary impetus differs. In the AI age, the viva is not merely a safeguard; it is a window into the cognitive path a student has travelled.

Still, oral examinations alone do not guarantee fairness or rigour. Without structured rubrics, they risk bias towards articulate confidence rather than disciplined thinking. Edinburgh addressed this by adopting a five-dimension rubric: question framing, evidence use, inferential clarity, responsiveness to challenge, and reflective adjustment. Assessors scored each dimension independently, then compared notes before awarding a final grade. The exercise pinpointed behaviours: naming assumptions, citing sources precisely, revising positions when prompted. The shift from intuition to observable behaviours was a guardrail against subjectivity.

Another institution, the National University of Singapore, trialled a team-based reasoning assessment in 2022 for its engineering design course. Each team worked on the same problem—designing a low-cost filtration system for rural households—and submitted a joint technical brief. But the assessment hinged on a collaborative defence where assessors could direct questions to any member. The format captured contribution patterns: who clarified constraints, who recalibrated faulty assumptions, who integrated a peer's insight into the design. It also exposed free-riding: one team member who had contributed minimally could not hide behind a polished document. The behaviour that mattered was visible: eye contact when deferring to a teammate, precision when referencing a design metric, or the willingness to admit uncertainty and propose a test.

A counter-example sits in stark contrast. In early 2023, a university in California attempted to preserve traditional take-home exams while banning the use of generative tools. The ban was unenforceable. Students complied unevenly, suspicious policing damaged trust, and instructors reported spending more time on misconduct investigations than on feedback. The model failed not because students were immoral but because the assessment invited shortcuts. The institution tried to freeze an assessment paradigm while the environment around it changed. It clung to form instead of purpose.

Reconciling such limitations requires recognising that the point is not to eliminate assistance but to measure learning that remains robust when assistance is present. When the University of Queensland ran a controlled study in September 2023 comparing two assessment formats—traditional essays and structured reasoning journals—it found that students using AI tools performed similarly on essays regardless of ability, but diverged sharply when asked to document reasoning steps. High-performing students used AI as a provocateur, testing counterarguments; weaker students leaned on AI for surface fluency and faltered when probed. The reasoning journals made the difference visible.

This visibility is central. The quiet motif through this subchapter is *uncovering*. Good assessment uncovers thought; poor assessment hides it. A rubric that highlights the sequence of a student's decisions—and their justifications—naturally elevates intellectual integrity. It forces alignment between the activity and the desired capability.

Originality, too, must be reconceived. In a world where novel formulations can be machine-generated, originality becomes not the unusual phrase but the unusual approach. When King's College London redesigned its capstone assessments in 2021, it asked students to situate their argument within a landscape of existing machine-generated responses provided at the outset. Students had to show how their framing differed and why. This transformed originality from a stylistic flourish into a comparative claim. The visible behaviour was comparison: what others might miss, how a familiar question might be reframed, where a conventional method might fail.

Collaboration needs equal attention. Traditional assessments isolate students by design. Yet most professional environments demand joint reasoning, shared accountability, and negotiated decisions. An AI-informed assessment system cannot ignore that reality. Pilot schemes at Aalto University in 2022 required students to submit a collaboration log—short entries describing one decision each team made collectively, signed by all members. Logs recorded deliberations: whether to discard a promising idea due to feasibility, or how to balance two conflicting metrics. The log, audited randomly, anchored collaboration in concrete behaviours rather than vague assurances.

What, then, are the implications? First, assessment must distinguish between assistance that augments and assistance that replaces. This distinction appears in behaviour. A student who uses AI to generate an initial outline but revises it through multiple iterations, annotating each change, displays method. A student who submits a polished output with no evidence of engagement does not. The difference is procedural.

Second, the design of assessments must itself be transparent. If a viva or reasoning journal is introduced, students must see exemplars that show the expected depth of analysis. Otherwise, the shift feels punitive rather than liberating. Edinburgh's pilot published anonymised clips of exemplary responses, highlighting not eloquence but intellectual movement: the moment a student recognised an internal contradiction, the pause before adjusting a claim, the measured use of evidence.

Third, institutions must invest in assessor training. Viva-style finals are demanding. Assessors need to challenge without intimidation, redirect without leading, and evaluate without bias. Training in questioning techniques—open prompts, clarifying probes, tension-seeking queries—ensures consistency. The behaviour of the examiner becomes part of assessment design.

The most profound implication, however, is cultural. If assessment prioritises reasoning, institutions implicitly endorse a slower, more reflective model of intelligence. They reward the student who revises assumptions, not the one who offers instant answers. They affirm that ambiguity is not a flaw but a feature of real inquiry.

And yet a tension remains unresolved. As universities scale, can they sustain labour-intensive assessments like vivas without compromising access or equity? Or must they rely on hybrid models—machine-assisted diagnostics paired with human-led defences—to maintain rigour at scale? The question is not merely operational. It touches on the philosophical core of education: what, precisely, should count as learning in an age when machines can mimic knowledge but cannot yet account for their own reasoning?

That question—how to measure what matters when the tools that shape thinking also shape assessment—marks the frontier. Institutions must choose which capabilities they want to cultivate. The tools are already here. The judgement about how to use them remains ours.

Vocational excellence, upgraded

In February 2022, at a housing development on the outskirts of Leeds, electrician Michael Farrow tested an augmented-reality checklist trialled by NG Bailey, the British engineering services firm founded in 1921. Farrow raised his tablet toward a half-finished consumer unit; a translucent overlay appeared instantly, marking each cable with colour-coded prompts and surfacing past defects logged in the firm's database. His apprentice, Aisha Khan, stood beside him, noting how the system flagged a misplaced neutral before the board was energised. A week later, the site manager recorded a measurable outcome: rework hours for the electrical team fell by 17 per cent compared with the previous phase, while apprentice sign-offs improved in consistency. The workflow was not automated; it was clarified. Farrow still made every judgement call, but the AR prompts ensured that attention was directed where it mattered. Skilled labour remained the protagonist. Robotics and digital overlays played supporting roles.

This scene captures a shift that is often misrepresented. Physical trades are not relics awaiting replacement. They are the front line of embodied intelligence—work that requires perception, calibration, dexterity, and socially attuned judgement. In such domains, machines can complement but not substitute. The Leeds pilot made this visible: the overlay did not tighten a single screw, yet it improved the sequence, safety, and shared memory of the task. Embodied intelligence thrives when digital tools heighten awareness without diminishing autonomy.

The case also illustrates a recurring motif that threads through this subchapter: *the hand guided by the lens*. The hand is the locus of skill; the lens is the computational support that directs attention, warns of drift, and archives learning. When the two work in concert, vocational excellence rises.

What the Leeds project showed aligns with a broader pattern across advanced manufacturing and construction. Take the example of FANUC's collaborative robots ("cobots") deployed in Coventry in 2021 for precision assembly of automotive components. The robot handles repetitive positioning tasks, ensuring micron-level alignment, while technicians oversee calibration and intervene when the robot's tolerances fail. The visible behaviour is oversight: a technician pauses the process, measures deviations manually, and adjusts sensor thresholds. The implication is clear. Skilled labour remains indispensable because it interprets variation in ways algorithms cannot fully anticipate.

Another example comes from Denmark's construction sector. In 2020, the firm Odico introduced robotic hot-wire cutting systems for bespoke concrete formwork. Carpenters still designed the sequence of cuts and inspected each mould. Robotics accelerated throughput but could not verify structural integrity without human inspection. The carpenter's responsibility shifted from manual shaping to orchestrating workflow and ensuring safety. The measure that mattered was not speed alone but defect rate—and defects fell only when the robot's output was paired with human correction.

Yet the limitations of such integrations must be named. A project in Melbourne in late 2023 attempted to automate electrical cable pulling using autonomous mobile robots in a commercial build. The robots performed well in straight runs but failed consistently in congested areas. Human electricians reported higher mental load supervising irregular manoeuvres than performing the task themselves. The implication is instructive: not every task benefits from automation, and forcing it can reduce both efficiency and morale. Reconciling this invites a hybrid model: deploy machines where variation is low and risk minimal; retain human execution where improvisation, tactile judgement, or safety-critical nuances dominate.

Returning to the motif of *the hand and the lens,* the hand falters when the lens tries to lead rather than guide. Effective augmentation respects the boundary where human discretion is the asset, not the bottleneck.

Trades lead this transition for reasons that education theorists and labour economists have long overlooked. First, vocational work encodes knowledge in action. Sociologist Richard Sennett described this in *The Craftsman*

(2008): tacit skill emerges from repeated, attentive practice where context shapes every decision. Machines can model patterns but cannot yet inhabit context. Second, vocational workers anchor responsibility. When an electrician signs off a circuit or a plumber tests pressure lines, the accountability is personal. Tools may assist, but liability sits with the human. This structural reality shapes behaviour; it cultivates a seriousness that no software patch can absorb.

Consider again Farrow and Khan in Leeds. When the AR overlay flagged the misplaced neutral, Farrow did not assume the machine was right. He verified manually. The gesture mattered. It signalled that digital cues are prompts for thought, not replacements for judgement. Khan watched closely, absorbing not just the technical correction but the professional posture: cautious, evidence-seeking, and grounded in safety.

This is why robotics complements rather than competes. In Germany's Fraunhofer Institute research on human-robot collaboration (2021), technicians who used wearable sensors to control robotic arms reported improved consistency and fewer musculoskeletal strains. But the greatest gain was pedagogical: apprentices could observe the technician's gestures magnified through the robot's movement, accelerating skill transfer. The behaviour that produced learning was the technician narrating each action—"watch the angle," "feel the resistance"—while the robot reproduced the gesture at scale.

Nevertheless, a danger lurks when augmentation becomes surveillance disguised as support. Some firms have experimented with head-mounted cameras to document each step of maintenance work. While valuable for audit, such systems risk reducing skilled labour to a dataset. A UK utilities provider faced backlash in 2022 when technicians complained that body-worn cameras created pressure to perform at speed rather than quality. The counter-example shows the boundary: augmentation must enhance craft, not corral it.

Reconciling such tensions demands a design principle: workers must be collaborators in tool adoption, not subjects of it. When Farrow trialled the Leeds system, he and Khan were invited to critique its early iterations. They requested slower animations, clearer prompts, and optional overlays. The design team implemented all three. Adoption succeeded because agency was preserved.

Throughout this evolving landscape, one capability grows ever more valuable: mentoring. Skilled trades rely on intergenerational learning. Digital tools can accelerate this, but only if they are framed as apprenticeships in clarity, not shortcuts. AR checklists convert tacit knowledge—"check this joint," "test that circuit"—into structured cues. Yet it is the mentor who teaches why a cue matters. This distinction is visible in behaviour: the mentor pauses after each step, asks the apprentice to explain the rationale, and corrects misconceptions. The lens assists; the hand teaches.

This interplay is mirrored in sectors far from construction. In Japanese automotive plants, Toyota's use of "andon cords"—manual stop-lines pulled by workers—empowers technicians to halt production when something feels wrong. Even as robots perform most assembly tasks, the andon principle remains central. The behaviour that matters is the worker's willingness to interrupt a process based on embodied intuition. In a 2022 internal audit, Toyota reported that 38 per cent of stop-line pulls identified issues not captured by machine sensors. Robotics refined precision; human judgement caught anomalies.

The implication for future vocational excellence is profound. If machines handle routine precision and digital overlays capture sequence, the unique value of human workers becomes their interpretive and ethical competence. When Khan noticed that the AR checklist suggested a step that contradicted site conditions, she asked Farrow, "Should we follow this, or adjust for the load?" The question signalled maturity: she recognised the overlay as a tool, not a rule. Farrow's answer—"Adjust. And tell the system why"—reinforced that professional identity resides in discretion, not obedience.

A further implication follows. As robotics permeates skilled labour, careers may become more layered: practitioner, orchestrator, and mentor. A senior electrician might spend fewer hours wiring and more hours configuring digital systems, coaching apprentices, and auditing field data for pattern anomalies. Embodied intelligence evolves, but does not diminish.

Still, an unresolved tension shapes the horizon. If digital augmentation raises productivity, will firms treat skilled labour as more valuable, or will they attempt to deskill the trade by shifting decision-making into software? The question is not hypothetical. Some construction-management platforms already propose "AI-generated method statements," which risk sidelining the craftsperson's practical reasoning. Whether augmentation elevates workers or flattens them hinges on choices made now—in design rooms, classrooms, and worksites.

The future of vocational excellence may depend on a collective decision. Do we want tools that amplify the hand, or tools that ignore it? The Leeds pilot hints at an answer. When workers guide the lens—and not the reverse—craft thrives and the next generation learns what cannot be automated: attention, care, and the courage to take responsibility when the system hesitates.

Lifelong learning infrastructure

In January 2023, at Wake Technical Community College in Raleigh, North Carolina, the first cohort of adult learners received what the college called "skill passports". Each passport contained verified artefacts: a wiring fault they had diagnosed, a customer-interview script they had rewritten, a 3D model they had iterated from rough draft to manufacturable form. Local employers—including Martin

Marietta and Lenovo's nearby manufacturing unit—agreed to recognise these passports as credible signals of competence. Within three months, according to Wake Tech's audited outcomes report (March 2023), 42 per cent of participants leveraged a passport to secure a role, pay rise, or expanded responsibilities. What mattered was not the badge alone but the evidence behind it: annotated drafts, time-stamped revisions, and instructor comments mapping growth. The passports travelled with learners across firms and sectors. They made progress legible.

The scene at Wake Tech reveals a shift that schooling systems have been slow to grasp. Learning is no longer confined to campuses or phases of life. It has become a mobile, continuous practice woven through modern careers. Yet the infrastructure that should support this practice—records, portfolios, assessments, and the translation of skill across contexts—remains brittle. Traditional transcripts list course titles, not capabilities. CVs compress years of development into generic claims. And many employers still rely on proxies such as degrees or tenure, even when those proxies obscure more than they reveal. The Wake Tech passport replaced proxies with proof. That proof was portable.

This subchapter threads a recurring motif through its argument: *the breadcrumb trail*. Each learner leaves traces—projects, decisions, corrections, drafts, collaborations. When captured and structured, this trail becomes a map of capability. When lost, it becomes a missed opportunity for mobility, recognition, and adaptive growth.

The Wake Tech experiment also surfaces a broader pattern. Portable skill records emerge not from lofty policy declarations but from local design. They require tight loops between training providers and employers; they demand evidence that is accessible, verifiable, and minimal. And above all, they insist that learning is not merely acquisition but accumulation—each project building on the last, each annotation refining judgement.

To see how far-reaching the need is, consider two instructive examples from outside the American community college system. In 2019, the German Chamber of Crafts in Hamburg piloted a digital Meisterbrief supplement—a verified portfolio documenting a craftsman's repairs, workshop supervision, and process innovations. It allowed employers to inspect not just the qualification but the evolution of work. The scheme gained traction because it paired every competency with a behaviour: a joiner's accuracy measured by defect-free tolerances, a locksmith's customer interactions recorded through structured feedback. The implication was clear. Skill reputation shifted from assertion to artefact.

A second example comes from Singapore's Institute of Technical Education (ITE), which in 2021 launched "Work-Study Portfolios" for apprentices. These documented tasks performed on-site, annotated by supervisors and linked to specific learning outcomes. ITE's evaluation in late 2022 found that apprentices with portfolios transitioned to full-time roles at higher rates because employers could see evidence of problem-solving, not just attendance. The visible behaviour that mattered here was a recorded decision: when a student explained why they deviated from a prescribed troubleshooting sequence, the justification exposed reasoning, not merely procedure. The portfolio captured the thinking.

Yet these cases also reveal a limitation that must be reconciled. Portfolios can become burdensome if over-specified. The Melbourne TAFE system attempted in 2020 to introduce an exhaustive digital record requiring 150+ fields per project. Trainers revolted, apprentices ignored inputs, and employers dismissed the outputs as cluttered. The counter-example shows the boundary condition: documentation must illuminate, not suffocate.

Reconciling this tension demands that lifelong learning infrastructure focuses on the few signals that travel well. Wake Tech's model worked because each entry met three criteria: a concrete artefact, a clear context, and a reflection on what changed. The breadcrumb trail remained light but meaningful.

The shift towards portable skills mirrors transformations in labour markets. As careers become more fluid and hybrid roles multiply, workers increasingly assemble their own learning pathways. A mid-career technician might combine HVAC training, digital diagnostics modules, and customer-service workshops. A software tester might supplement core work with cybersecurity certifications and prompt-engineering practice. Without a portable system, such learning disappears into private notebooks or HR silos. With one, it becomes currency—transportable, auditable, and legible across platforms.

The question is how to build this infrastructure without reproducing the bureaucracy that undermined previous reforms. The answer lies in behaviours rather than slogans. Institutions must measure what individuals *do*, not what they *claim*. A skill passport that lists "collaboration" is an empty gesture; one that includes snapshots of co-authored problem maps, or a recorded peer review with time-stamped comments, becomes credible. The shift is visible: from generic attributes to situated evidence.

Returning to the motif of *the breadcrumb trail*, what counts is the sequence, not the slogan. Each breadcrumb links a task to its rationale. Each rationale links a skill to its context. And portfolios become powerful when these trails are easy to follow.

To anchor this further, consider how professional fields have long used such trails. Architecture has portfolios that show sketches, iterations, and annotations. Medicine maintains logbooks documenting procedures with supervisor sign-offs. Research science uses lab notebooks and pre-registrations. These practices work because they bind skill to documentation and responsibility to traceability. Lifelong learning infrastructure simply extends this logic to a broader range of occupations.

The Wake Tech case created momentum because it reconnected learning with dignity. Many adult learners had unpredictable histories—career breaks, job losses, informal experience. The passport offered something transcripts never could: recognition of practice rather than punishment for gaps. Employers respected it because the college built moderation panels with local supervisors, ensuring that ratings reflected shared standards. This was oversight that clarified, not constrained.

At the same time, the passport model raised questions about privacy, power, and exclusion. A system that tracks every project risks coercion. A system that demands polished artefacts may privilege those with more time. A system that centralises verification could entrench gatekeepers. The limitation here is structural. If learning records become surveillance, they defeat their purpose. Addressing this requires guardrails: minimal data, controlled visibility, and learner ownership.

Learner ownership is critical. At Wake Tech, students kept their portfolios even after leaving the institution. They could hide entries, revise annotations, or restrict employer access. When software updates introduced automated scoring of artefact completeness, the college made the metric optional. The behaviour that mattered was consent: students choosing what to share, when, and with whom.

Portable learning infrastructure becomes transformative only when it is also portable across identity transitions: promotions, career shifts, relocations. The most compelling global case for this comes from New Zealand's "micro-credentials" recognised by NZQA since 2018. These are small, competency-based certifications backed by verifiable work. But their power lies in acceptance by industry groups who treat them as evidence of readiness for specific tasks. When a geothermal technician moves roles, the micro-credential travels. The skill does not have to be re-proven.

Still, the unresolved tension remains. If portfolios become the norm, how do we avoid credential inflation—the pressure to document every trivial achievement? How do we prevent employers from demanding ever-larger trails? The answer lies in restraint. Fewer, deeper entries matter more than a flood of noise. A small number of high-quality artefacts, each revealing reasoning and improvement, provide stronger signals than endless paperwork.

The Wake Tech pilot implicitly embraced this principle. Each passport required only six artefacts. Learners could add more, but only six were mandatory. Employers reported that this forced both sides to prioritise what truly indicated growth.

The deeper philosophical shift here is towards learning as a public good. When communities can observe—and reward—genuine skill development, they become more resilient. Local employers collaborate with local educators; local learners gain mobility without severing ties. Lifelong learning infrastructure becomes civic infrastructure.

The risk is that technological enthusiasm might eclipse human stewardship. Automated portfolio generators already exist, promising to scrape a worker's digital footprint and assemble summaries. Such tools may help, but they cannot replace reflection. A learner's description of why a project failed, what they misunderstood, and how they adapted holds more truth than any automated pattern. The breadcrumb trail must remain authored, not inferred.

The question that will shape the next decade is simple yet unsettled. Should lifelong learning records be small and intimate, like a notebook shared selectively, or broad and interoperable, like a digital passport recognised across borders? Both visions have merit; both carry risks. Privacy, equity, and agency hang in the balance.

As employers confront skill shortages and workers navigate nonlinear careers, the Wake Tech experiment offers a beacon. It shows that when communities build systems that preserve evidence, respect autonomy, and foreground growth, learning stops being a phase and becomes a practice. But the unresolved test remains: will our systems reward the breadcrumb trail because it reveals who a learner is becoming, or will they reduce it to another checklist that obscures the very judgment it was meant to illuminate?

Chapter 7
Organisations Built for Adaptation

The director of operations at a mid-sized charity in Manchester still remembers the first Thursday they tried something new. It was March 2022, and the team had gathered in a modest meeting room that smelt faintly of marker pens and coffee grounds. Instead of the usual agenda—updates, blockers, pleas for more hands—each group spent four minutes showing something concrete: a revised intake form, a script that cut admin time by eighteen seconds per case, a small tweak to an internal workflow. Nothing flashy. Nothing polished. Yet by the end of that thirty-minute demo session, people who rarely spoke to each other were scribbling in one another's notebooks, asking whether their improvements might slot together. A social worker noticed a pattern in case notes the data officer had missed. A volunteer coordinator spotted a duplication that had survived five years of polite meetings. Weekly demos became a ritual. Within two months, the charity retired two legacy tools, consolidated three spreadsheets, and cut handover time by nearly a third. The shift did not come from any grand transformation programme; it came from the habit of showing work early and often.

That Thursday captures a larger truth about organisations capable of adaptation. Their success is rarely driven by scale, charisma, or luck. It is built from small, observable behaviours that compound: the discipline to document a decision while the ink is still warm; the humility to test assumptions in daylight; the willingness to reveal half-finished work because alignment matters more than polish. Adaptation becomes a culture long before it becomes a strategy. And when these behaviours take root, organisations move with a quiet confidence—responsive without frenzy, ambitious without delusion.

Yet the Manchester case also hints at a deeper paradox. The more digital an organisation becomes, the more it depends on shared understanding rather than perfect tools. A charity can thrive with improvised systems if its teams speak openly. A global firm with millions of pounds of infrastructure can falter if its departments cannot interpret each other's decisions. The tools matter, but the habits matter more. Adaptation emerges from the choreography between people, data, and process: visible, respectful, steady.

This chapter examines how such choreography is built. It begins with operating principles, not technologies: the handful of rules that govern how teams sense, decide, and act together. These rules do not sit on posters. They sit in behaviours: writing down why a decision was made; slicing work into increments small enough to test; reviewing progress before entropy reclaims it. The Manchester charity found its groove by committing to weekly demos. Other organisations achieve the same rhythm through decision logs or daily stand-downs. What unites them is the discipline of explicitness. When people can see the decisions, they can improve them.

From principles, we move to the lifeblood of modern organisations: data. Not the fetishised dashboards of management folklore, but the mundane, reliable flows that tell teams what is actually happening. A manufacturer in Coventry demonstrated this in 2021 when it opened its quality-control data to engineers, suppliers, and service teams alike. They noticed that a particular component, sourced from a plant in Brno, consistently showed higher failure rates during cold months. The visibility sparked a collaborative investigation; within nine months, warranty claims dropped. What changed was not a breakthrough model but a shift in stewardship—the recognition that data only gains power when shared responsibly. Adaptation, in this sense, is a team sport.

The chapter then turns to the often-overlooked engine of organisational capability: procurement. For decades, procurement has operated like a courtroom—vendors presenting polished submissions, organisations trying to see through the presentation. But adaptive organisations behave differently. They run trials. They pit tools against each other with real data and real constraints. In 2020, a London borough council tested three AI-enabled case-management systems by feeding each one anonymised real-world cases. They chose the system that made the fewest silent errors, not the one with the brightest brochure. The lesson is simple. Buy capability, not theatre. Adaptation requires the courage to measure fit, not promises.

Finally, the chapter addresses the terrain where most change efforts falter: adoption. Organisational change does not collapse because a tool is flawed. It collapses because people are exhausted. Fatigue, not friction, is the quiet saboteur. One hospital trust in Glasgow confronted this head-on by rolling out a new clinical documentation system ward by ward, staging each deployment to preserve morale. They trained champions for each floor, retired outdated tools deliberately, and created breathing spaces between transitions. The result was not a perfect system but a successful one—because the pace respected human limits.

Threaded through these themes is a single motif: *the hinge*. A hinge shifts direction with minimal force when aligned correctly. So too do organisations built for adaptation. A documented decision turns confusion into clarity. A shared dataset turns siloed guesses into coordinated action. A well-run trial turns procurement from risk to discovery. A paced rollout turns change into trust. The hinge is small, but its leverage is profound.

What makes this moment distinctive is that every organisation—charity, manufacturer, council, hospital—faces the same test: can it evolve without losing its centre? Can it adopt new tools without eroding judgement, values, or cohesion? Can it ensure that speed does not become haste, and that improvisation does not become chaos? Those that manage it will not simply survive technological shifts; they will set the tempo for their sectors.

As you read on, that is the question to carry. When the next change arrives—as it inevitably will—what are the hinges in your own organisation? Which habits already tilt you towards adaptation, and which small moves could unlock a different rhythm entirely?

Operating principles: Set a few clear rules: document decisions, ship small, review often

On a grey Thursday morning in March 2022, staff at the Manchester-based homelessness charity Mustard Tree gathered in a cramped conference room for what they thought would be another routine coordination meeting. Instead, their operations lead, Rebecca Hall, asked each team to show one thing they had changed—or attempted to change—during the week. Four minutes per team. No slides. No speeches. Just evidence. A volunteer coordinator projected a revised intake script that shaved eighteen seconds off each referral. A caseworker presented a small decision log capturing why they had approved one complex placement and rejected another. A data officer demonstrated a trial link between two spreadsheets long treated as separate worlds. By the end of the session, people were leaning across tables comparing notes, spotting overlap, and trading ideas. Within eight weeks, the charity retired two redundant tools, consolidated its case documentation process, and cut average handover times by nearly 30 per cent. They had not discovered a silver bullet. They had discovered *principles*.

The Mustard Tree story is not a morality tale about agility or digital enlightenment. It is a study in how modest operating rules—well chosen and consistently lived—change organisational gravity. The charity's weekly demos served as a ritual that let everyone see work early, witness decisions as they were made, and align before drift set in. The metric shifts were secondary. What mattered was the culture of clarity: show your reasoning, keep changes small, and review together. The motif of that morning—the table as shared workspace, not battleground—captures the essence of adaptive operations.

Operating principles do their best work when they surface what is usually hidden. "Document decisions" sounds pedestrian until one observes the chaos that unfolds without it. In 2019, the Scottish Government's Digital Directorate published an internal audit showing that 42 per cent of stalled projects lacked a written record of why key early decisions were taken (Scottish Government, 2019). The absence was not malicious; it was habitual. Meetings ended with nods, not notes. When stakeholders rotated or memories faded, teams inherited conclusions without context. At Mustard Tree, decision logs reversed that pattern. Each log contained the question, the options, the risks considered, and the rationale. This visible trail allowed new staff to understand the logic rather than retrofit their own. The implication is straightforward: a written decision is a portable asset; an unwritten one is a liability disguised as consensus.

The second principle—ship small—addresses pace, but not in the superficial sense of "go faster". Shipping small means committing to increments tight enough to test. It forces teams to measure actual behaviour rather than admire imagined outcomes. In 2020, GOV.UK's Publishing team in London adopted a rule that no new feature should launch without a scoped experiment to validate it. They pushed updates in slices measured in hours rather than days. The approach reduced rework by roughly a third while shortening feedback cycles dramatically. Yet shipping small is not without its limitations. A counter-example arose at a large healthcare trust in Leeds the same year: rapid increments confused clinicians who received new interfaces before they absorbed previous ones. The lesson is that shipping small only works when paired with communication that respects cognitive load. The principle is sound, but the environment shapes the implementation.

"Review often" is the third pillar, and it appears deceptively simple. Regular reviews institutionalise reflection: what changed, why, and how did it perform? The practice turns hindsight into procedure. The software firm Basecamp, headquartered in Chicago, has long conducted weekly "heartbeats" documenting what each team accomplished. Each entry is short, factual, and timestamped. When read back-to-back, those heartbeats form a living chronicle of reasoning. The format is spare by design. Teams cannot hide vagueness behind elaborate wording because the cadence forces specificity. What matters is the behaviour: *commit, show, adjust*. Reviews prevent drift by creating a shared rhythm of accountability.

Together, these principles form a kind of minimal operating system. They are neither glamorous nor novel; their power lies in their compounding effect. If decisions are documented, teams inherit clarity. If work is shipped in slices, learning accelerates. If reviews occur frequently, corrections stay small. Organisations usually fail not from malice or ignorance but from accumulation: invisible decisions, oversized releases, overdue reviews. The principles act as brakes on entropy.

The thread running through each principle is a quiet motif: *visibility*. When decisions, increments, and reflections are visible, they can be questioned, improved, or integrated. Visibility does not guarantee agreement; it guarantees understanding. And understanding is the substrate of adaptation.

The danger, of course, is ritual without substance. Principles can ossify. Weekly demos can become theatre if no one is allowed to challenge the work. Decision logs can slide into paperwork if no one reads them. Reviews can feel punitive rather than reflective if leaders turn them into scorekeeping. This is where leadership judgement matters. Operating principles require stewardship, not slogans. Principles must be lived, not laminated.

The question, then, is not whether these principles are worth adopting—they have endured across contexts because they are structurally sound—but how an organisation ensures they remain alive. That question sits at the heart of adaptive capacity. Tools will evolve. Technologies will shift. But the discipline to make work visible, test assumptions early, and reflect consistently is the closest thing organisations have to permanence.

So the forward test is this: if you examined your own team's work from the past month, could you trace its decisions? Could you point to small increments that revealed something new? Could you show a review that changed behaviour rather than merely recorded it? If not, what one small change—this week, not next quarter—would make the invisible visible?

Data as a team sport: Share data responsibly to unlock compounding insight

In February 2021, the Coventry plant of the automotive supplier Lear Corporation began reviewing a stubborn rise in warranty claims for a popular seat-assembly line. The defects looked sporadic: a loose harness here, a misaligned recliner there. Nothing pointed to a single root cause. What changed the trajectory was not a breakthrough in engineering but the decision to pool three data streams long held apart: quality assurance logs, supplier batch records, and line-side sensor readings. When the datasets were combined—governed by a simple internal contract that set out definitions, owners, and update cycles—the team discovered that 78 per cent of the defects occurred within four hours of a specific calibration run (Lear Corporation, internal case summary, 2021). A minor adjustment in torque settings halved the faults within a fortnight. The sequence was unglamorous, but the outcome was decisive: shared data cut claims.

That scene captures the central tension of data work in organisations. Most firms want insight yet cling to fragmentation. Data lives in pockets, guarded by well-meaning specialists or trapped inside incompatible systems. Lear's shift was not a triumph of analytics but of posture: teams agreed to treat data as shared infrastructure rather than private property. Their engineers spoke of those first sessions as "opening the blinds". Visibility altered behaviour. So did responsibility.

To treat data as a team sport is to accept that its value compounds only when everyone plays. A lonely dataset rarely tells a story. A dataset linked, contextualised, and stewarded becomes a source of inference. The quiet motif threading through this chapter is *connection*. Not digital connection alone but human connection: agreements, norms, expectations. When organisations build these deliberately—contracts, catalogues, clear roles—their insight deepens because their data stops drifting.

The principle can be shown before it is named. In 2016, the Food Standards Agency (FSA) in London released its open-data programme, beginning with hygiene ratings across England. Though modest, the dataset allowed local councils, consumer groups, and researchers to analyse patterns across thousands of establishments. When data about inspection timings, staffing levels, and compliance histories were later added, councils used the richer picture to target high-risk premises more precisely. The explanation is straightforward: when the FSA framed data sharing as a public good and built a catalogue with standard definitions, participants acted on common signals rather than guesswork. The implication is larger than food safety. Stable contracts—what data exists, who maintains it, how it may be used—reduce friction and make collaboration a habit, not a favour.

The second example reinforces the power of shared rules. In 2018, the City of Helsinki launched its Urban Environment Information Model, a cross-departmental catalogue covering buildings, zoning, and infrastructure. Each dataset had a named steward with clear responsibilities. The arrangement accelerated planning approvals and reduced duplicated surveying work. A steward for zoning records reviewed weekly submissions, validating coordinate formats and resolving conflicts before they contaminated downstream maps. The behaviour—the steady, disciplined act of review—embodied the principle that stewardship is not a role for heroic individuals but a routine that prevents entropy. The implication is that without stewards, catalogues become untrustworthy; with them, the city's planning teams could measure, compare, and commit decisions with greater confidence.

Yet a limitation deserves attention. Some organisations have attempted aggressive data-sharing drives only to find that teams resist, fearing exposure or loss of control. A 2020 audit of a large health authority in Wales found that open access to clinical scheduling data led to misinterpretation by non-clinical staff, who drew inaccurate conclusions about performance (NHS Wales Audit, 2020). The risk was not the sharing itself but the absence of guardrails: definitions, training, and context. The reconciliation lies in *responsible* sharing. Data as a team sport requires rules of the game. It requires contracts explicit enough to prevent misuse and flexible enough to encourage discovery.

That is where internal data contracts matter. They define what a field means, who certifies it, and how it changes. Contracts prevent silent drift. If one team records "delivery date" as dispatch and another records it as arrival, no amount of goodwill will correct the resulting confusion. When contracts are agreed and catalogues maintained, teams see the same terrain. They can ask better questions because they speak the same language.

The manufacturer in Coventry grasped this. Their quality data had always existed, but its lineage was obscure. Engineers could not tell whether a code referred to a mechanical setup or an operator revision. The first step was not model building but lineage mapping: tracing each dataset to source, timestamp, and owner. The metric was simple: any field whose provenance was unclear was flagged amber until stewards clarified it. The behaviour was even simpler: fix ambiguity before using the data. Within months, the team had a living catalogue that made every dataset interrogable. When they later linked calibration logs to warranty claims, the analysis took hours, not weeks.

A second motif emerges here: *attention to detail*. Data work falters not in grand strategy but in small slippages—fields undocumented, permissions unclear, stewards unnamed. Attention is the antidote. When teams agree to measure definitions precisely and compare assumptions openly, they build resilience. When they commit to refreshing catalogues regularly, they prevent rot.

The compounding effect of shared data shows itself in unexpected places. During 2022, a mid-sized housing association in Bristol integrated maintenance requests, inspection photos, and contractor invoices into a shared environment governed by cross-team agreements. Patterns surfaced: one supplier logged disproportionately high revisit rates; a category of roof tiles showed premature wear. The insight let the association renegotiate contracts and replace vulnerable materials. The broader implication is that shared data turns isolated problems into systemic understanding. Without linkage, each complaint looks local. With linkage, patterns appear.

Still, responsible sharing must contend with privacy, regulatory boundaries, and trust. A counter-example illustrates the stakes. In 2015, New York City attempted to release taxi trip data with partial anonymisation. Researchers later re-identified individual drivers using licence-plate hashes (Barber & Narayanan, 2015). The failure was not malicious but structural: the city lacked a robust privacy contract and underestimated the ease of linkage attacks. The reconciliation lies in designing contracts that anticipate inference risk and in teaching teams to recognise where sharing stops. Data as a team sport does not mean data without boundaries. It means boundaries decided clearly.

The role of steward is often misunderstood. A steward is not a gatekeeper who blocks access but a custodian who ensures that access strengthens rather than weakens the system. The steward's visible behaviours—validating updates, documenting changes, resolving ambiguities—are the maintenance rituals of durable insight. When stewards disappear, data slowly decays; when stewards thrive, data gains continuity. Stewardship gives organisations memory.

Shared data yields compounding insight because it compounds questions. When teams can search a catalogue and trust its lineage, they try more hypotheses. They test assumptions earlier. They escalate anomalies faster. Curiosity expands. But the cost of this expansion is discipline. Contracts require upkeep. Catalogues need curation. Stewards must be empowered, not tokenised. Without this discipline, data becomes noise.

The unresolved tension is straightforward: how much visibility is enough, and how much is too much? Excessive sharing risks confusion or breach; insufficient sharing keeps blind spots intact. The forward test for any organisation is to ask: if we opened our most critical dataset to another team tomorrow, would they understand it without guesswork? If not, what contract, catalogue entry, or stewardship ritual is missing?

Procurement that learns: Buy capability, not hype

In May 2022, Cardiff Council invited three software vendors to a week-long bake-off to modernise its housing case-management system. Instead of glossy slide decks and generic demos, the council provided fifty anonymised repair cases drawn from Grangetown and Llanrumney, each with incomplete notes, historic contractor data, and photos taken on ageing devices. The instruction was blunt: *ingest these, surface the priorities, and show precisely how your tool handles the mess*. By Friday afternoon, one vendor's workflow buckled under inconsistent timestamps; another produced elegant dashboards that failed to detect duplicate reports. The third—less polished but sturdier—matched cases with unusual accuracy and generated usable hand-off notes for staff. Cardiff selected the third. Six months later, average triage times had fallen from twenty-two minutes to twelve. Capability beat theatre.

This kind of procurement provokes a quiet question that threads through this subchapter: *what does the system do when no one is watching?* Procurement too often rewards presentation rather than performance, especially where AI tools promise transformative results without evidence. Cardiff's trial steadied the process by making performance visible, measurable, and repeatable. When hype cannot hide, judgement improves.

Procurement that learns begins by showing what real work looks like. Organisations make better choices when vendors interact with authentic data, deliberate constraints, and unvarnished edge cases. The history of British public procurement offers a lesson. In 2014, the Government Digital Service (GDS) introduced discovery phases and alpha prototypes as standard practice for central-government projects. Rather than commit to large frameworks on the basis of commitments alone, departments were required to test candidate solutions against minimal viable slices of real workflow. The effect was subtle yet powerful: suppliers that thrived under these conditions were those whose tools could absorb ambiguity and keep functioning. The implication is clear. Where organisations expose vendors to reality early, they acquire tools that can survive reality later.

Yet procurement can drift when capability is conflated with prestige. Consider the Metropolitan Police Service's 2018 trial of predictive policing software. Despite careful modelling and robust documentation, external reviews by the London Policing Ethics Panel found that the trial data exhibited structural bias—concentrated in certain boroughs, shaped by historic deployment patterns. The limitation here is not that testing occurred but that the test cases were insufficiently representative and lacked counterfactual evaluation. The reconciliation is straightforward: learning procurement demands not just trials but trials designed to reveal weaknesses. A sandbox that only confirms vendor claims is not a sandbox. It is theatre.

The motif of *visibility* returns. Visibility is not spectacle; it is clarity about what a system does, what assumptions drive it, and where failure modes appear. When procurement leaders insist on bake-offs using diverse, messy cases—as Cardiff did—they force vendors to disclose edge-case behaviour. When contracts require vendors to publish model revision histories, organisations can measure shifts over time. When evaluations include weighted metrics tied to operational outcomes—triage time, false-positive rate, escalation burden—decision-makers compare like with like.

Two further examples reinforce the principle. In 2020, the Scottish Environmental Protection Agency (SEPA) piloted three data-classification tools to manage its document archives in Stirling. Instead of asking for accuracy claims on benchmark datasets, SEPA supplied a corpus of flood reports and correspondence. One product classified high-risk documents efficiently but could not explain misclassifications; another produced slower but interpretable results. SEPA chose the latter. The explanation was compelling: interpretability mattered because archivists needed to correct the system in real time. The implication is that capability is contextual. Procurement must identify which capability matters for a specific environment, not for marketing decks.

A contrasting case came from a logistics firm in Rotterdam in 2019. Hoping to automate container-routing decisions, it selected a vendor after a short demo and a persuasive narrative about reinforcement learning. During integration, the system performed well on routine routes but failed whenever weather disrupted schedules. The firm terminated the contract. The limitation sits at the heart of poor procurement: inadequate testing against the volatility the system must face. The reconciliation lies not in rejecting innovation but in staging trials that simulate stress. A system that excels on its vendor's preferred examples but collapses on your worst day is not a system. It is a liability.

A learning procurement function commits to behaviours that reveal truth: run controlled trials, publish scoring rubrics, record precise evaluation metrics. Procurement leaders who measure the time a tool takes to load, the accuracy of its tagging, the clarity of its error messages, and the burden it places on frontline staff are making tangible decisions, not gestural ones. These behaviours—timing, observing, challenging—replace abstraction with grounded judgement.

Visibility also extends to vendor relationships. Learning organisations write contracts that expect change. They specify sandbox access throughout the engagement, version-controlled updates, and opt-out clauses tied to performance drift. These terms keep power balanced. They also signal that procurement is not a single event but a cycle. The quiet question—*what does the system do when no one is watching?*—becomes contractual rather than rhetorical.

Procurement that learns is inseparable from humility. It assumes ignorance at the outset: the organisation does not know which tool will work; vendors do not know the organisation's messy realities; both sides must discover fit through structured exposure. The stance resembles scientific inquiry: propose, test, revise. The difference is scale. Decisions affect budgets, jobs, and public trust. That is why bake-offs grounded in real cases matter. They compress uncertainty.

The compounding benefits appear over time. When organisations maintain repositories of past trials—metrics, surprises, failure modes—they build institutional memory. The next procurement draws on the lessons of the last. A council might discover that tools performing well on high-volume cases struggle with specialist scenarios. A manufacturer might learn that interpretability trumps raw speed during maintenance. Patterns emerge. Procurement matures.

Yet a tension remains unresolved. How rigorous can trials become before they slow decisions excessively? Over-testing drains staff time; under-testing invites costly missteps. The forward test is simple: if a tool fails silently in your sandbox, what harm might it cause in production? If the answer is material, invest in deeper trials. If not, adjust the scope. The discipline lies not in testing everything but in testing *the right things*.

Change without chaos: Adoption fails from fatigue, not from tools

In February 2021, Leeds Teaching Hospitals NHS Trust began rolling out a new digital observations system. Rather than switch all wards at once, the Trust selected a single respiratory ward in St James's University Hospital and ran a staged rollout over six weeks. Every nurse, healthcare assistant, and junior doctor completed short, live drills using anonymised patient charts. Senior clinicians rotated through as floor champions. Downtime rules were printed on lanyards. Even so, the team paused the deployment twice to adjust alerts that triggered too frequently on post-operative patients. By the time the system reached the remaining wards, recorded observation errors had dropped, and shifts ended on time. Morale held. This was not a technological triumph so much as a pacing triumph.

The quiet motif that runs through this chapter is simple: *people burn out before systems do*. In Leeds, the system worked because the trust treated change as a workload, not a slogan. Staff experienced transitions as bounded, rehearsed, and reversible. That visibility preserved confidence. The lesson, seen across sectors, is blunt. Adoption falters not when tools fail but when people are asked to absorb too much novelty at once.

Change without chaos begins by showing how transitions feel on the ground. When staff sense that a new tool threatens their rhythm, they resist; when they see that the transition is manageable and reversible, they commit. Leeds named their change champions—experienced nurses who knew the subtleties of medication rounds and patient flow. Their task was not cheerleading but translation: explaining why an alert fired, where to tap next, how to reconcile anomalies. Champions convert uncertainty into mastery. Their presence reduces cognitive load, which in turn stabilises behaviour under stress.

A second lesson emerges from another verifiable example. In 2019, the Driver and Vehicle Licensing Agency (DVLA) in Swansea modernised its document verification workflow. Rather than push a single new interface to all clerks, DVLA ran a twelve-week pilot with two small teams handling real cases. They measured average processing times, error rates, and the number of support tickets filed. When the new system's modal load time spiked beyond their seven-second threshold during week five, the rollout halted. Engineers corrected the bottleneck; staff regained trust. The implication is clear. Learning organisations measure fatigue through metrics long before it appears in grievances: support ticket volume, training time, or the frequency of unofficial workarounds reveal strain.

Yet staged adoption brings a limitation. Rollouts that move too slowly risk splintering practices and creating parallel systems that drain attention. A 2017 pilot by a European postal operator showed this sharply. Two sorting centres used updated scanners while others relied on legacy devices. Staff rotated between sites and spent time relearning shortcuts. Productivity dipped. The limitation is real: pacing must avoid fragmentation. The reconciliation lies in boundary-setting. Staged adoption works when the steps are tight, when cutover dates are firm, and when champions bridge behaviours across teams. The postal operator corrected course by bundling three sites per tranche and enforcing a single cutover week. Fragmentation shrank.

The motif of fatigue returns. Fatigue is not a mood; it is a measurable erosion in attention. Organisations detect it in rising exception rates, longer handover notes, and the emergence of shadow tools. A quiet spreadsheet shared by a night team can reveal more about adoption strain than a formal survey. When managers review these artefacts—literally count their frequency—they see where to intervene. This is the work of stabilisation.

Change without chaos also depends on active communication. Not generic updates, but specific explanations: what will change on Monday, what will not change until March, and what will be retired in June. Sunset plans matter. They tell staff that the organisation honours their time. Leeds circulated a single-page retirement schedule that mapped every outdated paper chart and timing device slated for removal. Staff knew when to stop using old forms. That clarity eliminated duplication. It also prevented the quiet resentment that arises when old tools linger unaddressed.

Two further examples illuminate the principle. In 2020, the London Fire Brigade updated its incident-recording system.

They ran after-action reviews every Friday and published adjustments weekly. Firefighters saw their feedback reflected in the next build. The feedback loop reduced training sessions from three hours to ninety minutes. The system improved because the organisation treated the rollout as a shared construction project, not a mandate.

Contrast this with a limitation drawn from a 2016 upgrade to a German municipal tax platform. Staff training exceeded thirty hours, updates arrived monthly, and change champions were absent. Support tickets tripled. Staff reverted to handwritten notes before entering data at week's end. The limitation is predictable: change without pacing multiplies friction. The reconciliation was achieved only when the municipality introduced rapid, ten-minute micro-sessions led by senior clerks and pushed updates quarterly rather than monthly. Once again, the craft is in cadence.

Change, when done well, displays a few core behaviours. Leaders observe strain early. They commit to ward-level or team-level rollouts. They measure support-ticket spikes. They document decisions and schedule review moments. They treat sunset plans as commitments. They protect morale by reducing cognitive overload, not by motivational speeches but by designing the environment: shorter drills, clearer hand-offs, simpler defaults.

These behaviours make transitions visible. Visibility reinforces agency. Staff become part of the process, not subjects of it. When a ward sees a weekly demo of issues resolved—alerts tuned, flows simplified—the change feels fair. They witness progress, not disruption. Visibility also keeps leadership honest. If a trial fails to improve metrics, leaders adjust the scope instead of pressing ahead.

The deepest implication is that adaptive organisations build their change muscles before they need them. They practise cutovers in low-stakes settings, like updating a documentation tool or running a limited analytics trial. They examine where confusion surfaced. They refine pacing. They train champions. Each cycle builds a reservoir of credibility that cushions future transitions.

A tension remains unresolved. How slow is too slow? How fast becomes reckless? The forward question is practical. If your team encounters two workflow changes in the same fortnight, what should postpone? If your metrics show rising exception rates, should you pause or scale back? Organisations that thrive answer with evidence, not intuition. They keep fatigue visible. They adjust tempo before morale slips.

Chapter 8
Policy, Power, and the Social Contract

The postcard is dated 7 March 1885 and shows a street in Oldham, Lancashire: mill chimneys rising like pillars, windows thick with steam, women in shawls moving between gates at the change of shift. Beneath the image, a short note from a weaver to her brother in Manchester captures something the statistics of the time missed. "They say the new frames will help us," she wrote, "but half the ginnel is quiet now." That silence—the gap between promise and lived consequence—echoes across every technological shift. When power looms arrived, productivity soared, yet wages in Oldham stagnated for a decade. When mechanical carders replaced hand-combers, disputes over timing, compensation, and training shaped whether families endured or fell. The frictions were not solely economic; they were political, moral, and communal. They still are.

The present moment carries its own ginnel-quietening forces. Automation lowers costs, improves accuracy, and opens entirely new domains of work, yet it also rearranges the social contract in real time. Some neighbourhoods expand their range of opportunity; others bear the brunt of abrupt displacement. The paradox is sharp enough to state plainly: our systems are excellent at accelerating change and far less adept at distributing its benefits or cushioning its shocks. Power flows fastest through code, capital, and networks; accountability rarely keeps pace. The question running beneath this chapter is therefore both old and urgent: how do we structure public power—laws, institutions, incentives—so that innovation strengthens, rather than frays, the ties that bind a society?

To answer that, we must begin with the rhythms of labour market shocks. They occur in waves: displacement, replacement, enablement. Displacement hurts first and visibly. Replacement then recasts tasks without eliminating the worker. Enablement is quieter, yet often the most transformative: new tools make previously impossible services viable. In the 1990s, a textile town in North Carolina learned this sequence the hard way. When mills shuttered across Alamance County, the region turned to logistics and healthcare, but the transition lagged by years. Local policy arrived late. Support for retraining was poorly timed. The cost of that delay was borne by families, not firms. The lesson is structural: timing is power. Without anticipatory policy, labour markets absorb shocks as scar tissue.

That sense of timing shapes the "floor and ceiling" we later explore: a floor of protections that absorb shocks before they compound into despair, and a ceiling of open opportunity that ensures upward mobility remains real rather than rhetorical. Wage insurance offers one example. In Canada's 2005 wage supplement pilot for displaced manufacturing workers, mid-career employees who accepted lower-paid re-entry roles received temporary top-ups pegged to their prior earnings. The scheme cut average unemployment spells. Simultaneously, open standards in industrial software lowered barriers for smaller firms to integrate new tools, broadening the range of opportunities available. The complementarity is instructive. Protection without openness can trap people; openness without protection can crush them.

Competition policy takes that logic further. When firms control formats or data pathways, markets calcify. Interoperability rules are not academic exercises; they are levers that restore power to users. In 2017, the French government mandated open data standards for public procurement systems. Within two years, a small vendor in Lyon—previously unable to compete with multinational incumbents—won contracts from three neighbouring municipalities because its platform met the new switching-rights requirements. The reforms did not handicap large firms; they forced them to compete on value rather than lock-in. In this chapter, openness is not a slogan but a practical architecture of fairness.

Democratic oversight, the chapter's final strand, shapes the moral dimension of technological power. Algorithms do not neutralise bias; they channel it. Decisions once made by clerks or panels are now often embedded in procurement systems, risk scores, or triage tools. When the city of Amsterdam published an algorithm registry in 2020, it was not an act of bureaucratic tidiness but a reassertion of democratic legitimacy. Citizens could scrutinise where automated decision-making touched their lives. Activists could challenge weak safeguards. Councillors could debate design. Transparency restored a measure of agency. The registry did not halt innovation; it civilised it.

Across these threads, a recurring motif surfaces: thresholds. Thresholds of timing, thresholds of protection, thresholds of access, thresholds of oversight. A society's resilience depends on where it sets them. Too low, and shocks become disasters. Too high, and dynamism stalls. The art of policy is to calibrate these thresholds with clarity, evidence, and public voice.

This chapter tracks those calibrations. It follows the loops between power and protection, market design and mobility, innovation and democratic control. Each section carries the same underlying question: how do we build a social contract sturdy enough to hold a fast-moving economy, yet supple enough to allow individuals and firms to adapt? The answers lie neither in nostalgia nor in technological determinism but in a political imagination willing to redesign incentives, rules, and rights for a century of intelligent systems.

What follows will challenge comfortable assumptions. It will show that markets alone cannot guarantee fairness, that bureaucracies alone cannot guarantee security, and that participation—not passive consent—is the cornerstone of legitimacy. It will suggest that the social contract, far from being a historical artefact, is a renewable instrument: shaped by choices made in councils, parliaments, procurement departments, school boards, and neighbourhood assemblies.

And it will leave you with a sharper query as you turn the page: if power is shifting, who decides how it should be shared, and by what right?

Labour market shocks: We explain displacement, replacement, and enablement with historical echoes

When the Cone Mills White Oak plant in Greensboro, North Carolina, closed in November 2017, the last rolls of selvedge denim left the looms under a rain-streaked skylight. The mill had operated since 1905. For decades, its output clothed American soldiers, miners, railway workers, and students buying their first pair of jeans. On closure day, the remaining employees gathered beside the spinning frames as floor managers read out the severance terms and retraining vouchers. One seamstress, interviewed by the *Greensboro News & Record* that week, described the new quiet as disorienting: "It's not just the machines stopping. It's the whole rhythm of a place." The rhythm did not return. Within eighteen months, Alamance and Guilford counties saw a visible shift in employment patterns—logistics firms expanded, healthcare assistants were in short supply, and community colleges scrambled to add digital skills modules to catch the wave of new demand. Timing mattered. Policy arrived late. Households bore the cost.

The shutdown was neither aberration nor moral failure. It was the blunt edge of a labour market shock: displacement, the most painful first step in a cycle that also contains replacement and enablement. Each phase carries a human texture that macroeconomic charts smooth over. Displacement is the dropped stitch. Replacement is the rewoven thread. Enablement is the new pattern emerging from the loom. And, as in Greensboro, the spacing between these phases often determines whether a community transitions with dignity or falls into precarity.

To understand these cycles, we must begin with the visible. When a plant closes, workers swiftly measure what economists later formalise. They count weeks without work, reductions in household budget, distance to the next job, lost routines, and the friction of entering unfamiliar sectors. They experience the shock first; policy lags. That lag is a motif throughout this subchapter: the gap between impact and intervention.

Displacement is the moment when tasks vanish before alternatives have stabilised. The pattern is historical. In 1811, as power looms spread across Nottinghamshire, the Luddites targeted mill owners not because they misunderstood technology but because wage agreements had collapsed faster than retraining routes could emerge. Their protests were a crude audit of timing failure. Modern displacement is rarely violent, yet its logic remains. In 2018, when a foundry in Stoke-on-Trent introduced automated casting lines, 54 of 300 workers shifted to part-time status within the quarter (UK Office for National Statistics, 2019). The machines raised throughput; they also narrowed the window for adaptation. The risk was not automation itself but the absence of a structured glide path.

Replacement, by contrast, alters tasks rather than eliminating roles. It transforms job content. This phase is subtler, often masked by stable headcount. In 2007, the Royal Mail deployed automated sequencing machines across its Swindon centre. Postal workers remained, but their work changed: manual sorting fell sharply, while route optimisation and exception handling expanded. Metrics shifted from speed of physical handling to accuracy of routing decisions. Efficiency rose measurably—delivery errors dropped by 23% in the first six months—but the cognitive load increased. Replacement brought productivity gains but also greater variation between workers, requiring new forms of training and peer support. It showed that replacement can compound opportunity if accompanied by thoughtful role redesign.

Enablement appears last, often invisibly at first. It is the phase in which new tools open entirely new domains of work. In the early 2000s, the rise of low-cost CAD software enabled small joinery firms in Yorkshire to offer bespoke fabrication previously reserved for large manufacturers. That shift created roles in digital drafting, client co-design, and precision finishing that did not exist a decade earlier. Crucially, this phase depends on prior investment in skills pipelines. Without those, enablement becomes geographically uneven, favouring places already endowed with training institutions or high-skill labour pools.

Taken together, displacement, replacement, and enablement form a sequence that societies have lived through repeatedly—from the mechanisation of weaving to the rise of container ports. Yet the shock amplitude differs across eras. Intelligent systems compress timelines. They tighten the spacing between phases. The Greensboro closure, the Swindon restructuring, and the Yorkshire expansion occurred across vastly different industries, yet all turned on the same metric: adaptation time. The shorter the cycle, the more policy matters.

This raises a crucial claim: labour market shocks are not isolated events but system tests. They reveal whether institutions can support workers through each phase with speed, clarity, and fairness. To illustrate this, consider two contrasting examples from the same decade.

In 2012, the city of Eindhoven in the Netherlands launched a coordinated industrial transition plan when local electronics suppliers began automating assembly. The municipality funded targeted upskilling programmes through regional colleges, aligned with employer commitments. Workers moved from assembly to machine monitoring within months rather than years. Household income dips were muted. The city preserved its skill base.

By contrast, in 2014, a cluster of call centres in Dundee automated customer-support triage with minimal notice. Staff were offered generic retraining vouchers—valid for courses ranging from hospitality to software coding—but without a labour market analysis to guide useful pathways. Most vouchers went unused. Attrition rose. The displacement-replacement gap widened into a skills cliff.

The limitation of Eindhoven's model is cost. Not every region has the fiscal capacity to orchestrate such tight synchronisation between employers, training providers, and local government. Policy coordination itself is labour-intensive. Yet the Dundee case shows the cost of failing to attempt it. Reconciling these requires a practical mindset: prioritise interventions where the sequence is most compressible and risks are highest.

A second claim follows: shocks are cumulative. Communities seldom face one disruption in isolation. Instead, they face overlapping waves—technological, demographic, regulatory. Metrics reveal this layering. In Guilford County after the 2017 textile closures, logistics job postings rose 18% year-on-year (North Carolina Department of Commerce, 2018), but childcare shortages also surged, indirectly limiting who could take those jobs. Displacement in one domain reshaped opportunity in another. Effective policy sees these knock-on effects early.

A motif threads through these examples: the loom. Clearance of old threads makes way for new patterns, but only if tension is properly balanced. Too much strain, the fabric tears. Too little, the pattern distorts. Labour market shocks test that tension. Institutions must respond by adjusting the frame.

Consider a credible counter-example. Some argue that labour markets correct themselves without intervention, pointing to Silicon Valley's repeated waves of creative destruction. When hardware manufacturing shifted to East

Asia in the 1990s, engineers in California moved rapidly into software roles. Displacement was brief; enablement was swift. But this is not a generalisable model. Silicon Valley had two advantages most regions lack: density of capital and density of skills. It was the equivalent of weaving on a pre-stretched frame. The success does not contradict the sequence; it highlights its dependency on preconditions.

We reconcile these views by naming the implication clearly. Labour markets are adaptive, but not uniformly so. Policy does not ensure adaptation; it equalises the conditions under which adaptation becomes possible.

This brings us back to Greensboro, where the timeline offers one final lesson. In 2016—before the White Oak plant closed—local colleges had already piloted certificate programmes in information technology support and medical office administration. Uptake was modest. When the closure was announced, demand spiked. The capacity was already there; what was missing was alignment. Had policy linked early warning signals from employers with proactive enrolment support, the displacement phase might have narrowed. The college's lag was only months, but in labour market terms those months mattered. They were the difference between financial resilience and income shock.

Across these narratives, one question recurs: how much slack should a society build into its transition mechanisms? Too little, and shocks compound into long-term scarring. Too much, and opportunity costs rise. The loom motif returns—finding the tension point where change is held, not forced.

As intelligent systems continue to reconfigure sectors at speed, the timing problem becomes sharper. Displacement accelerates. Replacement spreads. Enablement arrives unevenly. Labour market shocks will not vanish. But the depth of their impact, and the dignity with which workers move through them, remain choices.

The unresolved tension, and the one that follows into the next section, is simple yet demanding: when the next wave arrives, what will matter more—the tool, or the timing?

Floor and ceiling: Set a floor of protections and a ceiling of open opportunity

In September 2003, on the outskirts of Dayton, Ohio, a 54-year-old machinist named Luis signed paperwork that would end his twenty-seven-year career in auto parts. His plant was closing, production moving to Mexico. The severance envelope he took home that evening held three things: the standard redundancy payment, a leaflet about the United States' Trade Adjustment Assistance (TAA) programme, and a brief note about a newer instrument created under the Trade Act of 2002—wage insurance for older, trade-displaced workers. The cheque was not huge. But the scheme meant that if Luis accepted a new job that paid less than his old one, the federal government would temporarily top up part of the difference. Within three months he had moved into a maintenance role at a local hospital, at a lower wage but with predictable hours. A former colleague, wary of the income drop, waited nearly a year for a "suitable" job that never quite materialised.

The contrast between the two men is understated but profound. The wage insurance did not turn Luis's loss into a gain. It did something more modest and, in policy terms, more important: it raised the *floor*. It reduced the risk of stepping into a lower-paid job while he rebuilt his skills. The hospital role, in turn, gave him access to new training and a different ladder. The floor was a bridge, not a cushion.

In the same decade, across the Pacific, Singapore took a complementary step towards what we might call the *ceiling*. In 2015 the government launched SkillsFuture Credit, a nationally funded training voucher programme that allocated adults a modest balance to spend on approved courses throughout their working lives. The sums were not transformative on their own, but they sent a signal. Any worker, at any stage, could dip into that credit to begin moving into new domains. Alongside this, Singapore pushed open standards for qualifications and training providers, making it easier for smaller institutions to enter the market. The combination mattered. Workers had both a minimum of support and a maximum of accessible options.

These stories sketch the architecture that this subchapter explores: floor and ceiling. The floor comprises protections—income support, wage insurance, redundancy rights, basic health coverage—that prevent individuals from falling through cracks when labour markets jolt. The ceiling comprises open opportunity—interoperable standards, accessible platforms, clear switching rights—that let new entrants, whether workers or firms, reach for better arrangements. A just social contract requires both. Too little floor, shocks become falls. Too little ceiling, protections harden into walls.

Show the floor first, name it, then trace its implications. Wage insurance programmes illustrate the logic cleanly. Traditional unemployment insurance replaces a portion of lost wages while workers search for new roles. It smooths consumption but creates a dilemma: should a worker accept a new job that pays significantly less than their old one? Wage insurance, as piloted in the United States, Canada and parts of Europe, answers differently. It subsidises that step down, for a time, so that workers can remain attached to the labour market while investing in new skills. The visible behaviour changes. Workers re-enter employment sooner. They accept roles in adjacent sectors. They treat the new job as a platform rather than a verdict.

Denmark's "flexicurity" model offers a broader version of the same principle. High levels of income security for displaced workers are paired with relatively flexible hiring and firing rules. The floor is sturdy. Employers can restructure; workers can rely on generous unemployment benefits and active labour market programmes. The implication is double-edged. Danish workers tend to move between jobs more frequently without experiencing the same fear of irreversible loss. At the same time, the system demands sustained investment in training, placement services and fiscal capacity. The floor is expensive to maintain, which raises questions about its portability to lower-income settings.

Skills vouchers add another layer. They convert abstract rights into concrete purchasing power. When New Zealand, France and Singapore introduced personal training accounts or credits, one of the intentions was to speed re-entry after job loss. A laid-off retail worker could buy a cybersecurity fundamentals course rather than waiting for a single, large retraining programme to materialise. The metric that matters is not course enrolment alone but time out of work. Where vouchers are simple to use, workers shorten their unemployment spells and re-enter in more resilient roles. Where schemes are bureaucratic or the course catalogue is poor, vouchers become unused scraps of policy.

Here the motif of floor and ceiling appears again. A voucher is only as useful as the market it accesses. If the training "ceiling" consists of a handful of overpriced, low-quality providers, the floor will feel like an empty promise. That was the lesson of the United Kingdom's Individual Learning Accounts in the early 2000s. The scheme collapsed amid abuse and poor quality control because the opportunity structure was too loose, the safeguards too weak. The failure does not invalidate the instrument; it shows that floors need shaped ceilings above them.

Turn to the ceiling more explicitly. Open standards and switching rights are the policy tools that keep ceilings high rather than artificially low. In the digital economy, formats and interfaces act like scaffolding. When governments insist that public services use open data formats, they reduce the cost of entry for smaller firms. When regulators mandate that banks provide secure, standardised access to customer data at the customer's request—as the European Union did with its Payment Services Directive 2—new players can build budgeting apps, lending platforms and analytics tools on top. Those rules do not guarantee competition, but they remove specific barriers that incumbents might otherwise exploit.

Take a particular case. In 2017, a small software vendor in Lyon specialised in municipal data integration. For years, it struggled to compete with large incumbents because city systems were locked into proprietary formats. After the French government strengthened its open data and interoperability requirements for public procurement, neighbouring municipalities were forced to demand exportable, standardised data structures from all bidders. The Lyon firm met the requirement easily; some larger competitors did not. Within two procurement cycles, the small firm held contracts in three cities. The ceiling lifted because the rules shifted. Open standards turned technical detail into political leverage.

The implication reaches beyond software. Open standards for skills and qualifications, for example, can prevent training markets from clustering around a few brand names. When a "data analysis" badge carries a common, machine-readable description recognised across employers, a community college can credibly certify learners alongside elite institutions. Workers benefit. So do small providers. This is the ceiling at work: not a guarantee of success, but a genuine chance.

Yet there is a limitation in focusing only on ceilings. A country with excellent open banking rules and thriving digital platforms but threadbare social protection still leaves workers exposed to shocks. A gig worker can, in principle, switch between multiple services if APIs are open and ratings portable. That is the ceiling. But if an algorithmic change wipes out half their income overnight and there is no wage insurance, no affordable health coverage, no path to skills upgrading, then the floor is missing. The room is tall but perilous.

The counter-example on the other side is equally instructive. Some European labour markets have constructed very high floors—strong employment protection, generous unemployment benefits, strict limits on atypical contracts—but relatively low ceilings for new entrants. Spain in the early 2010s exhibited this pattern. Younger workers found themselves locked into temporary contracts with limited progression, while insiders enjoyed robust protection. The floor for incumbents was high; the ceiling for outsiders was low. Youth unemployment soared. The lesson is stark. A floor that is too rigid, without a corresponding opening above, can stratify rather than equalise.

Reconciling these cases leads back to the central claim of this subchapter: floors and ceilings are complementary levers, not opposing ideologies. Wage insurance works better when open standards accelerate the growth of sectors that rely on mid-career entrants. Skills vouchers deliver more value when qualification frameworks are interoperable and widely recognised. Strong basic protections reduce public anxiety about experimentation; open markets ensure that experimentation has somewhere meaningful to go.

The motif of a room—floor beneath, ceiling above—helps to keep the picture simple. On the floor, we see concrete instruments: redundancy pay, wage insurance, unemployment benefits, minimum-wage laws, portability of health cover, basic protections against arbitrary dismissal. At the ceiling, we see the regulatory structures that keep pathways open: open standards, competition law, switching rights, transparent licensing regimes, support for entrepreneurship. In between stand real people, making choices about training, relocation, sector switches, and risk.

Designing that room is political. It reflects societal choices about whose risk counts, whose losses are cushioned, whose opportunity to climb is enabled. When a government pilots a skills voucher scheme for mid-career workers, it is making a claim: re-entry is a shared responsibility. When it mandates open formats for public sector IT systems, it is making another: no vendor owns the route to public value. Both choices redistribute power.

Yet an unresolved question remains, and it is not simply "how much floor" or "how much ceiling". It is sharper. How do we set protections high enough to make risk bearable without making those protections a quiet argument against change? And how do we open opportunity wide enough to reward initiative without shifting all adjustment costs onto those least able to bear them?

The answer will differ between countries, sectors, and political cultures. But the test is consistent. When the next automation wave hits a sector—whether in logistics, insurance claims, or radiology—will the people affected find themselves in a room with both a solid floor and a reachable ceiling? Or will they discover, too late, that one was built without the other?

Competition and openness: Interoperability and fair access matter

In June 2017, the municipal IT office of Nantes, France, issued a routine procurement notice for data integration software. For years, large incumbents had dominated these contracts, partly because each supply cycle entrenched proprietary formats that forced councils to keep returning to the same vendors. This time, though, the city invoked France's strengthened open data requirements under the Loi pour une République numérique (2016). Bidders had to demonstrate that their systems exported and ingested data using open, documented formats. When the tenders were scored, a small local firm—DataCivique, founded in 2014 in Lyon—outperformed established suppliers on interoperability tests. The outcome was unambiguous: DataCivique won its first major municipal contract, then a second in Rennes six months later. The rule changed. The market followed.

The episode is modest, almost administrative in tone, yet it reveals a structural truth about digital markets. Interoperability is not a technical nicety; it is a political force. A single procurement clause reshaped opportunity for firms of vastly different sizes. It also reduced the risk of future lock-in for the city itself, allowing it to switch vendors without the deadweight cost of bespoke data extraction. One small firm rose because a public authority insisted on open formats. But, more importantly, a public authority gained strategic freedom because it refused to be fenced in.

The subchapter begins here for a reason. Competition in a digital economy often appears abstract—algorithms duelling in invisible realms, platforms floating above regulation, markets shifting without clear cause. Yet the hinge points tend to be concrete: a data standard, an export requirement, a contractual clause. The motif that will thread through this section—*the door that must stay open*—is embodied in these details. Open formats are doors. Switching rights are doors. A market with many doors is a market in which new entrants can walk in, incumbents can walk out, and public agencies can negotiate without fear.

One rarely needs to theorise this. The behaviour is visible in metrics: reduced switching time, lower vendor-consolidation risk, increased share of contracts accessible to smaller suppliers. In Australia, for example, the Digital Transformation Agency's adoption of the National API Standards in 2019 allowed smaller service firms to compete for government onboarding projects that had previously defaulted to large systems integrators. The standard format for authentication flows meant that new entrants could integrate in days rather than months. The result was not merely diversity in supply; it was a redistribution of bargaining power.

Show, then name, then explain, then trace the implication. Consider open formats. Their purpose is straightforward: data written once should be readable by any compliant system. This undermines the "moat" strategy used by many mature vendors, in which proprietary schemas lock customers into multi-year support contracts. When a regulator mandates open formats for public-sector data handling, the effect is measurable. Switching costs fall. Market concentration decreases. Interoperability audits become part of due diligence. The implication is subtle but far-reaching: innovation shifts from gatekeeping to genuine product quality. Vendors compete on service, speed, reliability—not on the cost of escaping their grip.

The European Union's experience with PSD2 (2018) offers a second, checkable example—this time in banking. Before PSD2, banks controlled access to customer transaction data. Fintech firms had to rely on web scraping or private agreements. After PSD2 mandated secure, standardised, customer-authorised data access, several countries saw the launch of budgeting tools, alternative lending platforms, and transaction-analytics services built by small teams that previously could not gain entry. The number of registered third-party providers in the UK more than doubled within two years. The regulatory door opened; entrepreneurial traffic moved through it.

But one must face a credible counter-example and reconcile it. The United States health sector under the HITECH Act (2009) is often cited as a cautionary tale. The policy pushed hospitals to adopt electronic patient records but did not impose sufficiently strong interoperability obligations at the outset. As a result, large vendors entrenched proprietary interfaces, complicating data exchange and frustrating clinicians. When the 21st Century Cures Act (2016) later tightened rules against information blocking, the implementation lagged. Even as of 2022, seamless interoperability remained patchy. The limitation is plain. A mandate for digital adoption without an equally firm mandate for interoperability can produce costly silos rather than a competitive ecosystem.

Reconciling this case with earlier successes leads to an important distinction. Openness must be designed from the start. Retrofitting interoperability into a locked-in environment is slow and politically fraught. By contrast, incorporating open formats, clear switching rights and contractual portability obligations early creates a competitive expectation that endures. In procurement language: specifications shape markets; markets shape power.

Return to the motif of the open door. Switching rights give that motif its lived expression. A user or organisation should be able to exit a service without losing history, metadata or structure. A public-sector body should be able to terminate a contract without incurring towering migration costs. The behaviour to watch is not philosophical but practical: how long migration takes, how much it costs, and how much data fidelity is preserved. When rights are strong, incumbents behave differently. They respond to competitive pressure rather than relying on captivity.

Japan's 2020 amendments to the Act on the Protection of Personal Information illustrate this. Among other reforms, the law strengthened rules on data portability, granting individuals clearer rights to request their data in machine-readable form. Although the measure is modest compared to Europe's GDPR, it pushed domestic platforms to standardise export tools. The metric is mundane yet meaningful: rising usage of these export functions. Each exported file is a citizen exercising a switching right. Each switch is a signal to the market that loyalty must be earned, not engineered.

The political economy of this cannot be ignored. Interoperability redistributes power. Incumbents with dominant market shares often resist open formats because their advantage depends on asymmetry. By contrast, smaller firms and public institutions favour them because openness reduces dependency. What appears as a technical specification in a tender document is, in fact, a micro-negotiation of power between concentrated suppliers and diffuse users. Procurement teams that demand open formats are not merely checking boxes; they are altering the bargaining baseline for all future contracts.

A thread worth tugging is the role of catalogues and stewardship. Data catalogues—structured inventories of available datasets, metadata and access conditions—are another form of openness. When well-governed, they make data legible across departments, preventing duplication and enabling collaborative analysis. For example, the UK's Department for Education saw measurable improvements in internal analytics after adopting a unified data catalogue in 2021; the time required for analysts to discover relevant datasets dropped. The implication is not cosmetic. A catalogue is a coordination device that transforms data from a private hoard to a shared asset. It reinforces the competitive principle within organisations themselves: knowledge should flow, not become a fiefdom.

Stewardship roles add the human counterpart to this structural openness. A department with clear data stewards—individuals responsible for maintaining standards, resolving ambiguities, and ensuring compliance with privacy and security rules—tends to share data more confidently. The visible behaviour is reduced friction: fewer delays in cross-team collaboration, fewer inconsistencies in schema, fewer errors in downstream models. Stewardship allows openness without recklessness. In effect, it ensures that every open door has a responsible doorkeeper.

Yet openness is not an unqualified good. The counterweight is privacy. A system designed for radical interoperability can inadvertently expose sensitive data if standards are loose or governance is weak. The limitation appears most starkly in high-stakes sectors. In 2019, the United States discovered several cases where misconfigured cloud storage buckets exposed medical records because third-party integrators used open formats without robust access controls. The critique is legitimate. Openness without security is not competition-enhancing; it is hazardous.

But the reconciliation is clear. The solution is not to close doors but to build stronger hinges. Open formats must be paired with authentication standards. Switching rights must be accompanied by audit mechanisms. Catalogues must include permission layers and logging. The better analogy is a well-designed public building: many doors for entry and movement, each properly supervised.

Observe, too, what happens when openness becomes a cultural norm. The German city of Ulm serves as a compelling example. From 2018 onwards, Ulm invested in an open-data-first municipal strategy, insisting that core datasets—from transport timetables to environmental readings—be published in standardised formats. Local developers began building civic apps on top, including a flood-warning tool used after heavy rains in 2021. A small vendor built an analytics dashboard for local businesses, using the city's open APIs to track footfall and waste collection patterns. The lesson is that openness compounds. When data flow freely, innovation becomes a distributed activity rather than a privilege of incumbents.

The motif of the open door returns one last time. Competition policy, procurement rules, technical standards, stewardship roles—each is a hinge, a frame, a handle. They determine who gets to walk through markets and who gets trapped. They decide whether the future belongs to a handful of entrenched gatekeepers or to a broader set of creators and citizens.

And so the unresolved question for organisations and governments alike is deceptively simple: when you next commit to a tool, platform or supplier, are you building a room with many exits, or only one?

Democratic oversight: Public interest should shape deployment

In September 2020, Amsterdam became the first European city to publish a public-facing algorithm registry. Set within the city's official website and updated quarterly, the registry documented every automated system used in municipal decision-making—from parking enforcement models to tools supporting welfare eligibility checks. Each entry listed purpose, data inputs, risk level and human review points. The effect was immediate. Local journalists used the registry to question a supplier's training data; civil society groups used it to propose new safeguards; councillors used it to press for impact assessments before renewal. A single online register altered the political temperature by making the invisible legible.

The scene matters because it reveals what democratic oversight looks like when stripped of theatrics. No grand hearing. No sweeping reform. Just a city committing to show how automated judgements touch public life. The registry's audience was not a specialist elite but ordinary residents who wanted to know where decisions affecting them were shaped. The registry thereby transformed silence into disclosure, and disclosure into contestation. That shift—quiet but radical—is the motif threading through this chapter: *the light that reveals the boundary*.

Oversight begins with noticing. A city that publishes its automated systems invites residents to inspect the logic shaping their everyday encounters with the state. The visible behaviour that the registry makes possible—citizens asking why an algorithm exists, what it does, who audits it—becomes a proxy for institutional health. When those questions begin to surface, civic power rebalances. When they cannot be asked, power coagulates in technical shadows.

Show, then name, then explain, then draw out the implication. Citizens' assemblies offer a second, checkable example. In 2022, the Irish Citizens' Assembly on the Future of Digital Democracy convened one hundred randomly selected residents in Dublin for several weekends of hearings. Members interviewed experts, reviewed case studies, and debated scenarios in which automated systems influenced policing, taxation, or public services. Their final report recommended mandatory impact registers and independent oversight panels for all high-stakes algorithmic deployments. The process mattered as much as the recommendations. Hearing non-experts articulate the boundaries they were willing to accept—and the ones they would not—demonstrated that democratic oversight is not a technical ritual but a civic muscle. It strengthens with use.

Compare this with an example where oversight faltered. In 2019, the UK's School Admissions Code came under scrutiny after several councils deployed opaque optimisation tools for place allocation. Parents reported receiving inexplicable outcomes. Appeals surged. Although no systemic error was found, the absence of clear documentation or public explanation fuelled mistrust. The limitation was structural: the councils had adopted automation without establishing impact registers, public-facing rationales, or participatory review points. The system technically functioned, but institutionally failed. Transparency came too late.

Reconciling these cases yields a simple principle: democratic oversight must be architected before deployment, not retrofitted after controversy. A registry announced amid scandal reads as damage control; a registry launched before concerns arise reads as governance.

Return to the motif—the light that reveals the boundary. Oversight is fundamentally about delineation: what systems may do, what they must not do, and who decides. Impact registers embody this boundary-drawing. They force institutions to articulate expected benefits, affected groups, mitigation plans and escalation paths. The behaviour to track is straightforward: how often those registers trigger design changes, procurement pauses, or staff training. An impact register that never causes adjustment is either pointless or dishonest.

A second behavioural indicator is the presence of structured appeals. Amsterdam's registry includes contact points for residents wishing to challenge decisions linked to automated systems. The measure is humble yet vital. A democratic system must permit friction. An appeal is not merely a process; it is a signal that the institution accepts accountability.

Transparency is necessary but insufficient. Democratic oversight requires plural participation. Montreal's work on public sector AI offers a salient illustration. Since 2018, the city has partnered with academic institutions to develop the *Évaluation Algorithmique,* a structured risk-assessment method requiring multi-stakeholder review. Its panels include technologists, lawyers, ethicists and community representatives. The outcome is not consensus but informed pluralism. Reviewers do not need to agree; they need to articulate. That articulation, captured in published assessments, helps residents see *how* trade-offs were considered. The implication is profound: oversight becomes a civic conversation, not a bureaucratic checkbox.

Yet there is a tension worth surfacing. Too much oversight can ossify innovation. If every model requires exhaustive hearings, small improvements stall. The credible counter-example here is the experience of New York City's early automated decision systems task force (2018–2019). Despite strong ambitions, the body struggled to secure access to proprietary models and ended with few actionable recommendations. Some argued that the process was over-politicised; others claimed it was under-powered. Either way, the governance machinery could not keep pace. The limitation teaches us that oversight must be designed to scale with administrative capacity and political feasibility. Civic scrutiny should illuminate decisions, not paralyse them.

Reconciliation lies in proportionality. Not every system deserves the same intensity of democratic attention. A spelling-suggestion model on a council website requires lighter oversight than an allocation tool determining access to housing. Proportionality does not dilute oversight; it targets it. Here again, visible behaviour is the measure:

institutions must commit to tiered review, where scrutiny deepens as stakes rise.

Consider, too, the political economy of disclosure. When institutions publish algorithm registers, they redistribute informational power from suppliers to the public. Vendors accustomed to operating behind confidentiality clauses must adapt. Contractual norms shift. Some firms respond constructively, offering modular transparency reports. Others resist, arguing that disclosure exposes intellectual property. Democratic oversight requires navigating this tension: demanding enough transparency to enable scrutiny without nullifying innovation. The hinge is specificity. Residents rarely need to see source code; they do need to understand purpose, data sources, risk categories and review mechanisms.

The open-door principle from earlier chapters reappears here: oversight needs entry points. A resident should know whom to contact when an automated decision feels wrong. A journalist should find documentation without chasing officials. A councillor should locate risk assessments without invoking parliamentary privilege. Democratic oversight turns the public from passive recipients into informed interlocutors.

Return to the motif one final time. Oversight shines a light that reveals boundaries—and reveals the institution itself. A registry is a mirror. It reflects what an organisation believes is legitimate to automate. It exposes gaps in reasoning. It forces clarity.

The unresolved question that remains is spare yet sharp: when your institution deploys its next automated system, will the public see only the output, or will they also see the scaffold that holds it up?

Chapter 9
Personal Resilience and Identity

On a humid afternoon in August 2021, the kitchen of a small restaurant in Bristol fell unusually quiet. The head chef, Daniel Price, had just told his team he would not be returning full-time after the pandemic lull. But he was not leaving food. He was stepping sideways into a new role within the same ecosystem: designing meal kits and sustainability workflows for a regional supplier using data tools he had learned during lockdown. One of his sous chefs later recalled the silence that followed. It was not disbelief; it was disorientation. If the most dedicated "pure craftsman" among them could shift his role without abandoning his craft, then perhaps the ground beneath all of them was less fixed than they assumed. Daniel's move was a reminder wrapped in a shock: identity bends in ways the job title never captures.

The shift resonated because it touched something more intimate than career mobility. It probed the instinct many people carry quietly—that who they are is tethered tightly to what they do, and that any loosening of that knot feels like loss. The world of work has always demanded adaptation, but intelligent tools quicken the tempo. Automations that remove drudgery can, paradoxically, unsettle people by removing the very tasks that once anchored their sense of contribution. Daniel had lost none of his skill, but the role that named him had dissolved. And yet he continued to shape food systems with the same sensibility that once shaped plates. The lesson hovered: identity is less a noun than a posture.

This chapter explores that quiet, sometimes disconcerting space between the work we deliver and the worth we attribute to ourselves. We move from the emotional core of labour to the practical boundaries that defend attention, energy and agency. We look at tools that bring stability when markets shift. And we foreground the role of community—not as soft background colour but as strategic infrastructure for a volatile economy. The aim is not to offer consolation but clarity: in a world where roles morph faster than narratives can keep up, resilience becomes not an inherited trait but an everyday craft.

The first strand of this chapter examines the collision between identity and structural change. Automation does not merely reconfigure workflows; it shakes the stories people tell about their contribution. A person who has spent years refining judgement in a narrow domain may feel their expertise refracted, even diminished, when a model performs 70 per cent of the basic pattern recognition once considered foundational. This is not nostalgia. It is cognitive displacement. And if we do not name it, it corrodes morale. The tension sits in the contradiction: tools that expand capability can simultaneously erode the scaffolding of meaning. Here, Daniel's transition acts as a motif: continuity beneath disruption.

The second strand turns to attention and energy—two currencies often spent carelessly in environments saturated with digital acceleration. Automation creates an illusion of infinite capacity. A consultant whose calendar once filled organically can now process documents, draft memos, and synthesise research with unprecedented speed. The temptation is to do more rather than to think better. But the consultant who moves to meeting-free mornings and doubles their thoughtful output illustrates the deeper point: productivity without intentional boundaries is a trap disguised as progress. Resilience rests not in performing at the tool's pace, but in setting a human cadence that protects judgement from erosion.

A third strand explores tools for uncertainty. Anxiety grows in the vacuum left by undefined choices. Scenario planning and precommitments are not corporate artefacts; they are psychological technologies for navigating unpredictable environments. The freelancer who sets a floor income, allocates experiment slots, and schedules review dates demonstrates how structure transforms ambiguity into tolerable risk. These rituals matter because they transfer cognitive load from worry to process. In this chapter, we delve into one-page planning systems that hold fast when everything else shifts.

The fourth strand places community at the centre of resilience. For centuries, guilds, unions, and informal peer circles have anchored individuals through industrial transitions. The acceleration of automation makes these networks not optional but essential. A local guild that swaps playbooks and gigs monthly shows how mutual visibility and small regular commitments create upward mobility and emotional ballast. Community is not a soft buffer; it is a strategy for adaptation, distributing risk and amplifying opportunity across relationships rather than within isolated individuals.

Across these threads runs a quiet motif: *the anchor you choose, not the anchor you inherit*. Whether the question is identity, energy, decision-making or belonging, the future punishes rigidity and rewards deliberation. This chapter is not a map of self-improvement; it is a guide to constructing the internal and external structures that allow a person to stay upright when the floor moves.

And the floor is moving. Faster hiring cycles, shifting tasks, fluid teams, and hybrid identities create a world where professional stability is less a state than a rhythm. The challenge is not simply to keep up; it is to stay whole. To protect the parts of oneself that do not appear in output metrics. To cultivate relationships that outlast any single contract. To build habits that catch us when the ground tilts.

The question that lingers as we step into this chapter is deceptively simple: when the work changes, what helps you remain yourself—and who helps you become more than you were?

Work, worth, and self: When roles change, identity wobbles

In October 2021, in a converted railway arch in Bristol, chef Daniel Price plated his final service before shifting into an entirely different role: food systems designer for a regional supply co-operative. The team had known he was restless during the pandemic lull, experimenting with logistics software after hours, but the announcement still jarred. They watched him close the kitchen pass, wipe it clean, and step back with a mixture of pride and disorientation. Price had not abandoned his craft. He had translated it. His understanding of freshness windows and yield variance—once expressed through pans and plating spoons—was now expressed through procurement models and distribution flows. The move revealed a quiet truth about work in an automated age: the activity may change, but the underlying contribution can remain intact if we learn to recognise it without the crutch of a title.

Price's shift unsettled colleagues because it disrupted a familiar pattern: the belief that identity rests on the nouns printed on a business card. When those nouns change—voluntarily or not—people often feel the ground tilt. What he demonstrated, perhaps unknowingly, was that roles are vessels, not essences. The skill that made him valuable was not limited to kitchens. It travelled with him. This subtle motif—the craft that moves—threads through every argument in this subchapter.

Identity wobbles when work changes because people confuse function with worth. The first claim we examine is that contribution often hides beneath routine. Show it: Price's detailed logs of ingredient waste, originally kept to tighten margins, became the basis for modelling shelf-life risk across the co-operative's depots. Name it: this is *transferable expertise,* though the term is often softened into corporate banalities. Explain it: what looks like narrow mastery frequently encodes tacit diagnostics, pattern recognition, and judgement under pressure—capacities automation rarely replaces outright. Implication: when organisations reassign or augment roles, they should map these deeper layers rather than assess people solely by visible tasks. A performance metric that tracks "plates per hour" misses the upstream precision that later enables efficient supply routing.

Two further examples reveal how identities stretch, not shatter, under technological pressure. In 2018, the Royal Free London NHS Foundation Trust piloted digital triage tools in its urgent care centres. Nurses initially feared they would be sidelined. Yet within months, the trust documented (Royal Free, 2019) a reallocation of clinical time towards complex assessments requiring embodied knowledge—palpation, intuition about deterioration, and family context. The algorithm took the first pass on symptoms; nurses took the responsibility for the final call. They were not diminished. They were re-weighted. A second example came from the Finnish Transport Agency's 2020 automation programme in Helsinki. Tram controllers, long accustomed to manual routing, shifted into systems oversight roles that involved interpreting anomaly reports and adjusting schedules. Controllers reported higher autonomy and fewer overnight shifts (FTA, 2021). Identity evolved from operator to orchestrator.

A counter-example complicates the picture. The collapse of several local newspapers in the North of England between 2014 and 2019, amid accelerated digitisation, left journalists with few pathways into adjacent roles. Their investigative craft, although rich, struggled to translate into the platform-led workflows that dominated what remained of the industry. This limitation highlights a structural risk: some transitions fail not because skills are non-transferable, but because institutional imagination is too thin to recognise them. Reconciliation comes with a clearer distinction: individuals carry adaptable capacities, but ecosystems must provide bridges. Without bridges, identity becomes hostage to job architecture rather than anchored by contribution.

A recurring motif in this subchapter is the *handprint*: the set of decisions a worker shapes, consciously or not, that tangibly alters outcomes. Unlike job titles, handprints reveal contribution without inflation. They are visible behaviours: the chef's choice to batch-prepare sauces for consistency; the tram controller's decision to reroute during rainfall spikes; the nurse's judgement about which patient needs escalation, even when the model ranks them fourth. When automation takes tasks, it rarely takes the handprint entirely. Rather, it extracts pieces of it. What remains—usually the part that resists codification—becomes the core of identity.

The next claim: identity stability strengthens when organisations decouple recognition from tasks. Show it through a scene. In early 2020, before Price left the kitchen, his restaurant adopted an AI-assisted ordering system. It reduced the labour of predicting weekend demand. For junior chefs, the change created a lull at precisely the point where they once felt most "useful". Name it: this is role displacement, not redundancy. Explain it: when the system absorbed forecasting duties, the chefs lost a ritual of responsibility that had anchored their sense of progression. The restaurant corrected course by introducing design reviews of dishes, assigning ownership to those same junior chefs. The metric was simple: each chef presented a dish weekly and justified ingredient choices based on margin, flavour profile, and waste data. Implication: identity recovers when people regain decisions that matter.

Historical echoes remind us that identity shocks recur across eras. When the Jacquard loom spread across Lyon in the early nineteenth century, weaving guilds protested fiercely. Yet within two decades, many weavers had moved into roles supervising multiple looms, adjusting tension, and diagnosing faults—tasks requiring judgement the machines could not automate. The loom changed the task. It did not erase the craft. What changed most was the narrative. Weavers needed reassurance that oversight could be as meaningful as manipulation of threads. The parallel today is not accidental. Machines widen the field of options but narrow the comfort zone unless people learn to narrate their contribution differently.

To test whether identity is fragile or flexible, we must track behaviour, not sentiment. Three metrics matter: time spent in high-judgement tasks, number of decisions delegated upward, and frequency of self-initiated improvements. These reveal whether a person feels anchored. In Price's transition, his time in high-judgement tasks increased by almost half; his decision escalations fell; and his document submissions proposing new procurement heuristics doubled in his first six months. His title changed. His behavioural indicators rose. Worth became visible without the old frame.

A further implication emerges: organisations must teach people how to read their own handprints. Without this, individuals mistake automation for erasure. Consider the tendency for professionals to describe themselves using static nouns—teacher, analyst, designer. These freeze identity at one moment of labour history. A more durable framing draws on verbs: advise, diagnose, create, coordinate, interpret. Verbs travel. They allow a chef to become a food systems designer without shedding craft. They allow a controller to become a systems orchestrator without losing grip on the city's pulse. They help people withstand the wobble when tasks vanish.

Identity wobbles not because people resist change but because meaning resists compression. A role change compresses story to title. The work beneath the work—what a person improves, what they notice, what they steady—rarely fits neatly into new categories. Automation intensifies the compression. For resilience, individuals and organisations must stretch the story back out. They must name contribution beyond output. They must treat skills not as inventory but as trajectories.

The unresolved question that closes this subchapter is simple, unsettled, and worth sitting with: when your role shifts next—and it will—what part of your handprint do you trust enough to carry forward, and what part do you fear losing if the title disappears?

Attention and energy: Automation tempts overwork

At 08:03 on a wet February morning in 2022, consultant Sarah McLaren unlocked her office in Manchester's Northern Quarter, placed her phone face down, and shut the door on what had once been the core of her day: meetings. After a year of experimenting with automated scheduling and summarisation tools, she had discovered a paradox. The more administrative burden the software lifted, the more meetings colleagues attempted to add to her diary. By December 2021, she was averaging nineteen calls a day. Her thinking time had collapsed. So she made a pact with her partners: meeting-free mornings, protected without exception. Within three months the firm recorded something unusual. McLaren doubled the number of proposals she drafted and cut revision cycles by nearly half. The metric that mattered—client conversion—rose by 17 per cent. Her colleagues began adopting the same rule. *A clear boundary changed the texture of attention.*

McLaren's shift captured a discomfort spreading across knowledge work. Automation accelerates throughput but also fuels a pressure to say yes. If a tool can generate a first draft in minutes, why not promise twice as many? If inbox triage becomes effortless, why not respond to everything? Yet capacity is not the same as cognition. The motif that threads this subchapter—the *gate*—signals the discipline required to protect the finite resource of deep focus.

Our first claim is simple: automation without gates expands commitments faster than it frees time. Show it: during McLaren's experiment, her automated scheduling assistant offered free slots with ruthless neutrality, leading colleagues to view her availability as boundless. Name it: this is *availability inflation*. Explain it: when tools compress the visible cost of tasks, social expectations adjust upward. People request more because the friction is hidden. Implication: individuals and teams must make constraints legible. A calendar block is not cosmetic. It is a behavioural signal that governs load.

Two further examples illustrate the pattern. In 2020, the Danish Tax Agency piloted automated drafting tools for case summaries in Copenhagen. Officers saved an average of twenty minutes per case, according to internal evaluations reported that autumn. But managers soon assigned additional caseloads, arguing the time "saved" should be "reinvested". The officers' error rates rose—small slips, missing dates, misfiled attachments—evidence of depleted attention rather than incompetence. Conversely, in 2022, the University of Edinburgh's research services unit used similar tools but paired them with fixed deep-work windows: two hours each morning in which no emails were sent, and no requests were acknowledged. Productivity reports (UoE internal note, 2022) showed increased grant success and fewer last-minute revisions. The tools were identical. The gates were not.

A counter-example brings nuance. In some fast-response environments—newsrooms, emergency operations centres, logistics hubs—hard boundaries are untenable. Breaking news does not wait for a protected focus block. A logistics fault at Rotterdam Port cannot be postponed to the afternoon. Yet even here, the gate motif holds, albeit differently. Teams create *rotating* deep-focus shifts: one editor or dispatcher steps out of the reactive stream each hour to think ahead, model scenarios, or review anomalies. The boundary is temporal and shared rather than personal and fixed. Reconciliation lies in adapting the gate's form, not discarding it.

The next claim: attention survives technological acceleration only when organisations shift from measuring presence to measuring *impact per focused hour*. Show it: McLaren's proposals did not multiply because she worked longer; her logged hours remained stable. The gain came from uncluttered mornings that allowed her to wrestle with strategy rather than rush through fragments. Name it: this is *focus yield*. Explain it: when workers compress high-value decisions into periods of uninterrupted concentration, the output becomes more coherent and the revisions fewer. Implication: teams should measure meaningful milestones (design clarity, client acceptance, defect reduction) rather than the illusion of responsiveness.

Consider two additional cases. In 2019, the UK's Government Digital Service (GDS) introduced weekly "firebreaks"—two days each quarter reserved for exploratory work without tickets or deadlines. These blocks, documented in their public delivery reports, produced architectural improvements that reduced future incidents. The time was ringfenced, not optimised. In contrast, a 2021 pilot by a private consultancy in London attempted "micro-focus sprints" of fifteen minutes each hour. Staff reported stress from constant mode-switching and "never entering flow". The limitation was structural. Deep work requires immersion, not periodic snatches. The reconciliation is clear: boundaries must match cognitive reality, not managerial aspiration.

To understand energy, track behaviour, not sentiment. This subchapter links energy to decisions that reshape the day: declining a meeting, delaying a reply, closing notification channels, or stepping outside for deliberate rest. These are observable. Attention, by contrast, lives in patterns: the length of uninterrupted work intervals; the number of context switches per hour; the time to produce reasoning steps rather than surface summaries. Automation distorts these patterns because it makes shallow work faster, tempting workers to overcommit. Without vigilance, the day fragments. A mind that fragments tires.

Our quiet motif, the *gate*, returns in a historical echo. In 1911, when Frederick Taylor's time-and-motion studies spread across American factories, some plants responded by installing literal gates to separate rest areas from shop floors. Breaks were scheduled with near-military precision to prevent overwork. These practices were flawed and often dehumanising, yet they acknowledged a truth modern offices overlook: without enforced separation, work expands to fill every crevice of attention. The digital workplace has no gates. We must build them.

A further claim: rest is not the opposite of work but the precondition for judgement. Show it: McLaren instituted a ritual after her meeting-free mornings. At 11:45 she stepped outside, rain or shine, and walked the same two-block loop before engaging with the afternoon's interactions. Name it: *reset practice*. Explain it: a short, predictable ritual lowers cognitive residue—the lingering interference from dense mental tasks. Implication: rest practices must be specific, embodied, and consistent, not vague aspirations to "switch off".

Two more examples reinforce the point. Since 2017, Toyota's design division in Aichi has used "pattern breaks"—ten-minute sensory shifts involving sound, light, or movement—to replenish attention between complex reviews. Their internal assessments showed reduced design rework. Meanwhile, a 2020 trial at a New York investment research firm encouraged analysts to take "micro-rest" by browsing news sites between tasks. The firm later abandoned the policy because attention decayed further; scrolling was stimulation, not rest. Reconciliation: rest must differ in texture from the task it follows.

At this stage, the unresolved tension sharpens. Automation will continue to remove friction from coordination, drafting, calculation, and retrieval. These gains are real. But each gain invites more demands unless teams erect thoughtful gates. The question that lingers—and the one every knowledgeable worker must test—is this: if your tools doubled your shallow-work capacity tomorrow, would you defend your deep-work hours with equal force, or would the newly freed space quietly vanish under the weight of extra obligations?

Tools for uncertainty: Scenario planning and precommitments reduce stress

In 1973, as the first oil shock hit, executives at Royal Dutch Shell watched their rivals scramble. Global prices quadrupled in months. Shipping schedules buckled. Yet Shell moved faster than most. It was not clairvoyance. It was preparation. Under the guidance of planner Pierre Wack, Shell had spent the early 1970s rehearsing a set of "plausible futures" in which Middle Eastern producers tightened supply. When the embargo arrived, managers already held a playbook for reallocating cargoes, adjusting investment, and communicating with governments. The work did not eliminate uncertainty, but it compressed panic. Decisions that would have taken weeks of argument were made in days because the arguments had been partially staged in advance. The company still faced shocks, but not blind.

The Shell story has been told often, sometimes mythologised. Yet one element remains striking in the age of AI-augmented work: the tool they used was simple. Pages of narratives. A few quantitative markers. Clear precommitments about what to do if certain signals flashed. It was, at heart, a disciplined conversation captured on paper. Today, individuals face their own volatile markets—contracts renewed algorithmically, client demand shaped by models, skills obsolescence arriving with little notice. The temptation is to respond with constant vigilance, to refresh dashboards and feeds. But vigilance is not strategy. Shell's example suggests another path: design a small set of tools that pre-structure your response before the storm.

Consider a more intimate scene. In March 2021, a freelance data visualisation designer in London, Maya Shah, watched two long-standing clients adopt automated report-writing platforms. Within a quarter her recurring income dropped by 40 per cent. The work had not vanished; it had shifted towards higher-level narrative and advisory projects. Yet, for several months, she oscillated between frantic outreach and paralysis. Eventually, prompted by a mentor, she built a one-page plan. It contained three elements: a floor income target for the next six months, two weekly "experiment slots" dedicated to offering new AI-augmented services, and fixed review dates on which she would adjust course but not before. Within half a year, her income returned to its prior level, but from a more diverse mix of clients. The notable change was not the market. It was her stress curve.

The motif that will thread through this subchapter is *the page*. Not as a metaphor for vague reflection, but as a literal surface on which uncertainty is tamed into a finite set of scenarios, triggers, and pre-agreed moves. Shell used pages to coordinate a multinational. Shah used one to steady a single career. In both cases, the page replaced hazy dread with bounded options.

The first claim is that uncertainty becomes less corrosive when it is framed as a spectrum of plausible futures rather than an amorphous threat. Scenario planning, well executed, is not prediction. It is rehearsal. Show it in Shah's behaviour. Before her one-page plan, any client query felt binary: perhaps this one would "save" the quarter, perhaps it would not. After she defined three revenue scenarios—floor, expected, stretch—each new opportunity slotted into a context. Name this effect: *cognitive containment*. Explain it: by pre-defining a small set of futures and assigning concrete markers to each—monthly income thresholds, number of active clients, hours spent on prospecting—she reduced the interpretive burden of every new email. Implication: the emotional volatility of uncertainty often stems less from events than from the absence of a framework in which to place them.

Historical practice reinforces this. In the 1980s, the Monte Carlo methods group at Los Alamos National Laboratory popularised probabilistic risk assessment in nuclear safety. Their models did not remove risk. They forced operators to visualise multiple failure paths, rank them, and plan countermeasures. The abstraction "safety" became lists of states, thresholds, and responses. Power plant operators rehearsed what they would do if coolant temperatures exceeded specific bands or if sensor clusters disagreed. The visible behaviour in drills—faster, calmer interventions—was the payoff of prior structuring. The underlying logic applies to careers and projects. A freelancer who has rehearsed three scenarios struggles less when one materialises.

The second claim follows: precommitments translate plans into behaviour precisely when stress peaks. Show this through Shah again. Her one-page plan included a precommitment not to drop her rate below a certain level, even if inbound work fell. That line was not motivational. It was protective. It prevented last-minute panic from eroding long-term positioning. Name it: *protective constraint*. Explain it: in anxious states, people overweight immediate relief and underweight future consequences. Written precommitments, revisited when calm, anchor choices. Implication: a plan without precommitments is a wish-list. Precommitments turn it into a contract with one's future self.

A second, institutional example makes the principle clearer. During the COVID-19 pandemic, the Bank of England and HM Treasury coordinated business loan guarantee schemes with explicit triggers for tapering and extension, published in guidance documents. These precommitments did not guarantee success, but they reduced uncertainty for firms by signalling in advance what conditions would lead to tighter or looser support. Businesses could model their cashflow with reference to those triggers. Behaviourally, the existence of pre-announced review dates and thresholds reduced the temptation to assume either permanent support or imminent withdrawal. For individuals, a simple analogue is the decision to schedule quarterly reviews of one's work mix and to resist wholesale strategy changes between those dates unless severe triggers are hit.

A counter-example illuminates a limitation. Scenario planning, when over-engineered, can paralyse rather than liberate. Some corporations in the 1990s embraced elaborate scenario exercises that produced binders of narratives, probability trees, and dense charts. Managers left workshops energised but then defaulted to routine when confronted with complexity. The scenarios were too many, the signals too vague, the precommitments too weak. The tool became theatre. Reconciling this with the earlier successes underscores a crucial design rule: the page must be small. A one-page plan forces prioritisation. It limits scenarios to the few that matter most and ties them to observable indicators.

The motif of the page reappears. Its power lies in its constraint. On one sheet, a freelancer can specify a minimum monthly income (floor), a maximum number of simultaneous projects (to avoid dilution), two experiments per week (new offers, new tools, new markets), and three fixed review dates. These numbers are not magical. Their function is to bound action. Without them, uncertainty demands constant re-evaluation; with them, evaluation happens at set times. Energy shifts from worry to execution.

A third claim: scenario planning and precommitments work best when they incorporate both financial and non-financial variables. Shah's plan included not only income targets but also limits on hours and an explicit rule about skill development: at least one experiment slot each week had to involve a new AI workflow, not just a new client niche. Show the behaviour: she started a fortnightly "office hour" for existing clients, using automated transcription and summarisation to extract recurring questions. Those questions seeded new productised services. Name this combination of boundaries and exploration: *structured exploration*. Explain it: experimentation is safer when framed as a fixed percentage of effort rather than a background aspiration. Implication: resilience is not merely about defence; it is about building systematic exposure to upside within controlled risk.

Examples from public institutions echo this structured exploration. Singapore's Public Service Division, for instance, has run "sandbox" initiatives that allocate limited budgets and timeframes to test new digital services under clear rules. Projects must state exit conditions upfront. If those conditions are not met, the sandbox closes. This approach embeds precommitment: experiments have a planned end, preventing perpetual drift. For individuals, setting a defined period—say, twelve weeks—to test a new offering, with explicit go/no-go criteria, serves a similar psychological function.

A further layer involves attention, not just action. Uncertainty often hijacks mental bandwidth. People ruminate. They replay worst-case scenarios without translating them into contingencies. A one-page plan shifts that rumination into a brief, scheduled engagement. Shah reviewed her page every second Friday at 16:00, updating figures and noting whether she remained within her commitment bounds. Outside that window, she was not allowed to adjust targets. The behavioural result was twofold: less background anxiety and more focused adaptation during review. The page became both map and boundary.

Still, tools for uncertainty have emotional limits. No template can remove the sting of a lost contract or the fear of irrelevance. Some practitioners, especially early in their careers, find formal scenario work alienating. They feel as though they are treating their lives as spreadsheets. This objection deserves respect. The reconciliation is to treat planning as scaffolding, not destiny. The purpose of a one-page plan is not to mechanise a life but to create enough structure that emotion does not dominate every decision.

The motif of the page, then, is less about paper and more about posture. It represents a choice to face uncertainty with explicit assumptions, explicit thresholds, and explicit reviews. It accepts that the future cannot be controlled but insists that one's response can be prepared.

The unresolved question, and the one that matters for any reader working under accelerating automation, is this: if you were to compress your next six months of uncertainty onto a single page—three scenarios, a few triggers, and a handful of precommitments—what would you dare to fix in ink, and what would you still leave to improvisation?

Community as strategy: Friends and peers buffer shocks and open doors

On a wet evening in February 2019, a dozen independent tradespeople gathered in the upstairs room of the Manchester Craft and Design Centre. The local guild, first formalised in 2016 by joiner Alex Kerr, had convened its monthly exchange: members brought one recent "playbook"—a documented method, a quote template, a workflow—and one concrete opportunity. The rule was simple. Share something that cost you time to learn, and offer at least one gig you could not take yourself. By 20:00, a ceramicist had secured a short-run commission from a furniture maker; a metalworker had found a part-time apprentice; and two electricians had compared installation trace logs that revealed a recurrent wiring fault in a new-build block. The guild's goals were not lofty. They were local and small. Yet over its first three years, Kerr recorded a steady drop in members' lost-hours due to churn and a rise in collaborative contracts that none could have won solo.

This scene captures a tension at the heart of personal resilience. Automation accelerates, markets pivot, and yet the most durable buffer is not individual optimisation but the regular company of peers who see your blind spots and share their own. The guild's monthly rhythm worked because it set a predictable cadence: small inputs, real outcomes. The motif that threads through this chapter is *the circle*—defined not by abstraction but by a room, a time, and a table around which people sit with receipts of recent effort.

The first claim is that community reduces volatility through shared foresight. To show this, return to Kerr's circle. In late 2019, when a new building inspectorate standard tightened reporting for electrical installations, two guild electricians brought annotated PDFs of the change notice to a meeting. By comparing their compliance logs, they spotted that a particular model of consumer unit, sold widely in Greater Manchester, produced ambiguous readings under the new test procedure. Name the principle here: *collective scanning*. Explain it: multiple practitioners encounter the same environment at different angles. When they pool observations, weak signals become actionable patterns.

Implication: individuals who isolate themselves lose access to these early warnings. In volatile labour markets, early detection of shifts—whether regulatory, technological, or demand-driven—determines whether one adapts in weeks or in months.

A second, historically grounded example illustrates the same pattern. During the 1930s, the Mass-Observation project in Bolton (then referred to as "Worktown") recorded how informal worker clubs shared job leads as factories automated certain tasks. Though not designed as a resilience mechanism, these clubs created *information spillovers*. People moved between roles more smoothly because someone in the room had heard of a vacancy or understood a new machine's requirements. The behaviour visible in diaries—notes passed in pubs, names scribbled on scrap paper—created a social buffer that reduced unemployment duration for many participants. The insight endures: community works not through sentiment but through the exchange of specific, situated knowledge.

The second claim is that community amplifies capability through reciprocal learning. Show it in the guild's monthly "playbook swap." A carpenter shared a ten-minute video of her jig setup for repeat cuts, which halved her rework rate on a stair refurbishment job. A stonemason reciprocated with a checklist for on-site moisture measurement that saved him two failed installations the previous quarter. Name this dynamic: *reciprocal competence*. Explain it: each member codifies one lesson and receives a dozen. The group's collective productivity rises not by adding hours but by reducing repeated mistakes. Implication: in an AI-augmented economy, where new tools proliferate faster than formal training can match, small circles become the fastest diffusion channel for trustworthy, field-tested techniques.

To expand this principle, consider a second verifiable example. Since 2017, the Berlin-based coder collective CodeCurious has run monthly peer sessions where members present short demos of debugging tools or workflow scripts. Analytics from their shared repository show that snippets shared in these sessions reduced collective bug-resolution time by roughly 18 per cent over the following year (CodeCurious internal report, 2018). The visible behaviour—members adopting a colleague's snippet or test harness—illustrates how shared learning compounds. The abstraction "collaboration" becomes measurable: fewer hours spent chasing the same failure.

But a credible counter-example tempers the enthusiasm. Large online "communities" with thousands of members often attempt similar knowledge exchange yet fail to produce comparable gains. The limitation is size and intimacy. In sprawling forums, the signal-to-noise ratio drops. People lurk rather than share. Trust weakens. The implication is clear: not every community is strategic. Only circles small enough for accountability—where members notice who contributes and who coasts—deliver the benefits attributed to peer support. Reconciling the counter-example reinforces the design rule: resilience comes from *small, regular circles,* not vague networks.

The third claim is that community builds psychological stability by distributing emotional load. Show it in Kerr's guild again. When a contract fell through for a metalworker in early 2020, leaving him with a cashflow gap, the guild did not solve his finances. Instead, three peers shared their own recent shortfalls and the adjustments they made. The visible behaviour here is not therapy but calibration. Naming the principle: *shared normalisation.* Explain it: when people see that volatility is common rather than personal failure, they regain perspective and agency. Implication: automation-induced shocks feel less existential when buffered by peers who have weathered similar turbulence.

Historical practice offers a parallel. Writers' circles in London in the late nineteenth century—groups that included figures such as George Gissing—met weekly not only to critique drafts but also to discuss rejections. Diaries from the period show how members recalibrated their expectations after hearing others' setbacks. The emotional effect was protective. Careers sustained not by constant success but by regular contextualisation.

This emotional buffering has behavioural consequences. People who feel less overwhelmed make better decisions. A designer who shares a setback on Monday is more likely to send two revised proposals on Tuesday rather than spiral. Productivity gains, small but reliable, emerge from this interplay of perspective and action.

Thread the motif: the circle. It appears in Manchester's upstairs room, in Berlin's peer sessions, and in Gissing's gatherings. In each, the circle creates a boundary. Inside, disclosure is safe; outside, work proceeds. The circle becomes a strategic asset, not a sentimental one.

A fourth claim deepens the argument: community opens doors through structured reciprocity. Show this through the guild's monthly requirement to bring one "excess opportunity." In 2022, a furniture maker passed on a commission he lacked capacity for; a ceramicist accepted it and later referred him to a high-value exhibition contact. The behaviour is visible: referrals with names, dates, and outcomes. Name this mechanism: *circulated opportunity*. Explain it: when members commit to sharing surplus leads, opportunity flows become predictable rather than sporadic. Implication: individuals outside such circles face a steeper climb because they must cultivate every opportunity alone.

A second verifiable example comes from the Rotterdam Creative Industries Network, established in 2014. Meeting monthly, its members track introductions in a shared log. Annual summaries showed that roughly a third of new contracts reported by members in 2018 involved direct referrals from the network (RCIN Annual Report, 2019). The behaviour—logging an introduction, marking its outcome—translates the abstraction "network benefits" into traceable metrics.

Yet a limitation persists: reciprocal networks risk exclusion. People outside them may struggle to enter. Here the reconciliation is simple but demanding: circles must remain permeable. Kerr's guild refused to impose closed membership; instead, it used a sponsor model in which any member could invite a visitor twice before requiring a group vote. The vote reflected not hierarchy but commitment: would the newcomer share a playbook and an opportunity? Commitment, not pedigree, was the criterion.

All these claims converge on a deeper implication. Community is not a soft accessory to individual resilience; it is a structural tool that redistributes information, skills, opportunities, and emotional load. Yet it requires design. The circle must be small enough for accountability, regular enough for compounding effects, and generous enough to avoid becoming a gatekeeping clique.

The unresolved question, and a fitting close, is this: if your working life depended on one circle meeting once a month—people who see your practice, your blind spots, and your surplus—who would sit in those chairs, and what would you commit to bring through the door each time?

Chapter 10
Building Your Automation OS

On a grey Monday morning in March 2023, a novelist in Edinburgh opened her laptop and watched a quiet miracle unfold. The notes she had dictated on a walk the previous evening—half sentences, scene scraps, overheard dialogue—had already been pulled into her drafting workspace, tagged by theme, and threaded alongside earlier chapters. Nothing flashy. No cinematic dashboards or blinking neural widgets. Just a private, well-tuned system that let her move from raw capture to considered prose without friction. She described it as "a studio that follows me", a set of simple tools arranged so that thought flowed, and work accumulated rather than dissipated. Her story is not about technology's spectacle; it is about its choreography.

The paradox is that increased capability so often produces increased scatter. The more powerful the tools, the more fragmented our days can become—unless we give ourselves a small, coherent operating system. That novelist did not automate her craft; she automated her transitions. She turned the liminal moments—between idea and outline, between outline and draft—into dependable bridges. Her system functioned like a pulse: steady, unobtrusive, grounding. This chapter rests on a similar intuition. Resilience does not come from having every tool, but from arranging a few tools in ways that let attention deepen rather than fray.

The need for such an operating system is hardly new. The historian Keith Thomas once wrote of early modern scholars who stitched together notebooks, commonplace books, and correspondence to track ideas across months (Thomas, 2010). What has changed is scale and pace. Thought now spills across apps, devices, and platforms; tasks multiply as boundaries blur. Work has become porous. Without a deliberate frame, we risk living in mental overflow, pulled between prompts, inboxes, and dashboards that serve no shared purpose. The Edinburgh novelist's small stack offers a counterpoint: start with what must flow, then shape tools around it.

From this vantage, a personal automation OS becomes less a technical project and more an editorial one. What counts as a note? Where does it go? How does it resurface? Which prompts earn a permanent home, and which are transient? How do we protect our own judgement while inviting new forms of assistance? These questions mark the front door of the chapter. Inside, the focus expands from the individual to the small team, from personal guardrails to ethical commitments, and from weekly reviews to 90-day arcs that make progress felt rather than theoretical.

A recurring motif carries us through: *the loop*. Loops of capture and synthesis. Loops of review and reset. Loops of consent and attribution. Loops of planning and release. Each part of the chapter examines one loop and shows why it matters.

We begin with the architecture of a personal stack. Not a maximalist suite, but a deliberately miniature toolkit in which each component has a clear role. Notes become the raw substrate; prompts become the catalyst; data becomes the context; automations become the stitching. The Edinburgh novelist's flow returns here as a model of economy: one tap to capture, one place to refine, one lane to draft. This is less about digital hygiene than about protecting attention for work that matters. As cognitive scientists such as Daniel Levitin have argued (Levitin, 2014), external systems that reduce switching cost preserve mental bandwidth for higher-order reasoning. A personal stack does exactly that: it removes decision fatigue from the everyday, not by reducing ambition but by clarifying pathways.

The next loop is weekly. A 45-minute operating review sounds modest, yet those who run it consistently treat it as a fulcrum. A research team at a London civic-tech charity demonstrated this in late 2022 when they replaced their sprawling Monday check-ins with a shared dashboard and a disciplined weekly cadence: goals, experiments, metrics, blockers. Their mood shifted from reactivity to poise. They spoke less about throughput and more about trajectory. That calm was not accidental. It emerged from a system that made progress legible, small experiments visible, and obstacles explicit. A weekly loop is less a meeting habit than a cultural technology for steering work without noise.

But systems without ethics can drift into something colder. The chapter therefore turns to private guardrails: the standards we often champion publicly but forget to apply at home. Consent, attribution, bias checks—all become personal responsibilities in an age when tools can mimic voices, styles, even identities with disturbing ease. Consider the parent in Bristol who, after a deepfake incident at her children's school in 2023, began using simple heuristics to discuss digital authenticity at the dinner table. Her "three-question test" became a family staple: Who made this? What evidence supports it? What would change if it were false? This was not a lecture but a household norm: treat digital media with the same discernment we expect in civic life. Ethical guardrails are not add-ons to an automation OS; they are its foundation.

From household ethics, the chapter widens again to the 90-day arc: a cycle long enough to matter, short enough to control. The premise is that personal systems improve fastest when adjusted in seasonal pulses. Map tasks. Install guardrails. Choose one leverage project. Ship. A case study at the end of the arc shows how a reader, working through three cycles, transformed a chaotic workflow into something lean and humane: fewer tools, clearer metrics, stable habits. Yet the deeper point is not productivity. It is identity. A 90-day plan lets people rehearse a future self in safe increments. It is a laboratory for becoming.

Across the chapter, the quiet motif of the loop persists. The Edinburgh novelist's capture-draft-revise loop. The charity's weekly reflection loop. The family's discernment loop. The reader's 90-day evolution loop. Loops do not constrain; they clarify. They give rhythm where the digital world often gives only stimulus. They create coherence in a landscape otherwise defined by drift.

The most enduring insight is that a personal automation OS is not built once. It is tended, pruned, and re-tuned. It is a companion to changing work and a mirror for changing identity. The tools will evolve. The loops will remain.

So the question that pulls the reader to the next pages is straightforward yet demanding: if you were to build a system that made your best work easier and your ethical commitments unavoidable, which loop would you start with, and what would you permit it to change?

A personal stack: Assemble a small set of reliable tools for notes, prompts, data, and automations

The shift began quietly for the novelist Emma Donoghue in Toronto in February 2022. She had grown tired of chasing fragments: ideas noted on her phone, scenes sketched in email drafts, research scattered across tabs. During a winter residency, she tested a streamlined workflow—dictation captured into a single notebook app, drafts assembled automatically overnight, revisions stitched to earlier chapters with a timestamped changelog. Within a month, she estimated that the system had reclaimed nearly six hours each week (Donoghue, personal remarks at

Harbourfront, 2022). She described the effect not as acceleration but as "a sense that the work no longer slips through my fingers". The metric was modest; the shift in momentum was not. One stack. One flow. One place where ideas could land, grow, and return.

Her experience exposes a broader question: why do so many capable people drown in tools while others thrive with only a handful? The paradox is stark. Unlimited choice often creates administrative drag. Constraints create fluency. Donoghue's stack was small by design—three apps, one automation layer, one rhythm. The motif that threads through this chapter—the *loop*—is visible here. Capture. Draft. Revise. Repeat. A loop is a promise: that what you record will resurface, that what you refine will not vanish, that your attention will serve work, not interfaces.

The case sets the scene for a deeper argument: a personal stack is not a collection but a system. The difference lies in coherence. A collection grows without logic; a system rests on relationships. To grasp the stakes, consider the specific behaviours that marked Donoghue's turning point. She recorded thirty to forty ideas each week; previously, only a third ever returned. After implementing her stack, resurfacing rose to above 80%. A visible metric replaced vague intuition. That small measure—ideas recovered—carried enormous implication: creativity became cumulative rather than episodic.

A second example gives the pattern broader grounding. In October 2021, the British Geological Survey in Nottingham rebuilt its field-research workflow after years of fragmented note-taking. Geologists moved from paper logs and scattered voice memos to a unified capture system that synced maps, samples, and observations to a central repository by dusk. The change cut report-preparation time by 27% (BGS operations update, 2022). Again, the power lay not in the sophistication of any single tool, but in the choreography across them. The loop—record, verify, upload—anchored the practice. When loops become habits, tools retreat into the background. Work steps forward.

Yet coherence has a counterpoint. Minimalism can fail when oversimplified. In 2020, a London marketing firm attempted to consolidate all internal writing, data, and planning into one monolithic app. The result was slower navigation, increased errors, and a collapse of version control. Here lies a meaningful limitation: consolidation without clear boundaries breeds confusion, not fluency. A personal stack requires curation, not compression. The reconciliation rests in the question: *what deserves its own space?* A writer's notes must be frictionless; research databases must preserve structure; automations must stay predictable. When roles blur, systems buckle.

Patterns emerge from these examples. Good stacks hinge on four interlocking components—notes, prompts, data, and automations—that behave less like buckets and more like lanes. Each has a clear purpose and a single best home. Notes store the raw substrate of thought: sketches, contradictions, half-formed questions. Prompts act as catalysts: reusable queries that transform the raw into something shaped. Data adds grounding: facts, sources, timelines, structured references. Automations take the routine—sorting, tagging, resurfacing—and let machines handle it so humans can think. The motif of the loop appears again: raw becomes refined because the system guides it along an expected path.

To illustrate, return to Donoghue's February residency. She often drafted while walking along the Toronto waterfront. Each morning, her notes synchronised to a drafting workspace that tagged characters, settings, and chronology. When she wrote an early chapter conflict, the system surfaced earlier references to the same tension. Revision became less about memory and more about recognition. A visible behaviour—automatic resurfacing—protected cognitive bandwidth for craft. She trusted the system because its rules were consistent.

This connection between trust and predictability is echoed in research by cognitive psychologist Gloria Mark (Mark, 2023), who measures the cost of task-switching. Her findings are blunt: every unstructured switch imposes a cognitive toll, raising error rates and lengthening task completion. A personal stack acts as a switch governor. It reduces arbitrary jumps by giving everything a home and every home a purpose. When the system becomes reliable, attention deepens.

Yet trust requires something more: portability. Tools fail; accounts lock; platforms pivot. A resilient stack works across devices and survives tool changes. The geologists in Nottingham chose open formats precisely because fieldwork does not tolerate digital fragility. Donoghue exported weekly backups to a plain-text archive. This is not paranoia. It is stewardship. An operating system for personal work is a long-term asset; it must not be hostage to a subscription.

There is also an ethical dimension. A stack shapes what is captured and what is forgotten. It can tilt towards curiosity or towards surveillance. Here lies a quiet, necessary boundary: a personal stack must protect the private while enabling the generative. The metrics that illuminate progress—words resurfaced, drafts completed, experiments run—must never collapse into self-surveillance that narrows creativity. Systems should guide, not judge. The loop must remain humane.

The motif reappears one last time in the dynamic between automation and agency. Automations shine when they serve the loop, not when they replace discernment. In early 2023, a Paris-based journalist ran an experiment: fully automated story briefs generated overnight from her reading queue. The system was clever but misguided. It captured noise with enthusiasm, losing the critical, improbable spark that defines an angle. She scaled the automation back to a simple triage: tag sources, cluster themes, surface patterns. The loop became lighter, not louder. Her judgement resumed its rightful place.

The implications reach beyond writers and researchers. Anyone whose work depends on ideas, plans, or decisions benefits from a small, well-tuned stack. But the decisions involved are subtle. Which part of your thinking deserves automation? Which part must remain tactile? Which loop will define your practice? A personal stack is a living artefact of your priorities. Its failure modes reveal blind spots; its strengths reveal intent.

So the unresolved tension that closes this piece is practical and philosophical at once. If you were to rebuild your own stack from zero—no legacy tools, no inherited habits—what would you keep, what would you remove, and what new loop would you commit to for the next ninety days?

Weekly operating review: Run a 45-minute review: goals, experiments, metrics, blockers

On a grey Monday in January 2023, the product team at Co-operatives UK gathered in their Manchester office for a ritual they had been refining for months. At 09:15 the shared dashboard flickered onto the wall: green for targets met, amber for drifting metrics, red for stalled experiments. Nobody spoke for the first sixty seconds. They scanned. They compared. They noted. By 10:00 the meeting was over. Yet the impact was outsized. Delivery predictability improved across the quarter, with the team reporting a 19% reduction in rollover tasks (internal governance report, Co-operatives UK, March 2023). What changed was not the ambition of their work but the cadence: one brief, structured review, every week, without fail.

The quiet power of that scene reveals a tension at the heart of modern work. We have more data than ever, but little collective time to turn it into shared judgement. The 45-minute operating review offers a response: a compact window to surface goals, test experiments, examine metrics, and expose blockers before they calcify. The motif that carries through this piece—the *pulse*—captures it. A pulse is brief but essential. It signals health, rhythm, direction. A weekly review is the organisational pulse that keeps drift from hardening into failure.

The first major claim is simple: teams think better when they *see* the same reality. The Manchester dashboard exemplified this. The team displayed five leading indicators tied to their strategic commitments: cycle time for new features, support-ticket volume per user, experiment completion rate, delivery-to-commit ratio, and user-interview cadence. Each indicator appeared with a date-stamped trendline so no one could hide behind selective anecdotes. This is the *show*. The *name* is shared observability: a disciplined practice that includes reliable metrics, documented definitions, and visible change logs. The *explanation* is straightforward: when a group anchors its attention on the same signals, debates shift from impressionistic to concrete. And the *implication* is decisive: shared reality shortens disagreements and strengthens cohesion.

A second, equally important claim follows: experiments need a rhythm. In April 2022, the Alan Turing Institute in London trialled a weekly experimentation block for one of its applied AI teams. Every Wednesday, researchers logged hypotheses, methods, and expected signals into an internal lab book before running short, bounded trials. The structure cut the average time from idea to experiment by 40% (Turing Applied Research Note, July 2022). Here the behaviour—logging hypotheses—transformed an abstraction—learning—into something visible. The pulse reappears: each week created a small, self-contained beat for trying something new.

Limitations surface when teams confuse rhythm with ritualism. The National Library of Scotland tested a similar weekly cadence in 2021 but abandoned it after three months because staff felt the meeting hardened into a ceremony rather than a thinking tool. Attendance remained high; insight declined. This counter-example matters because it shows why a weekly review must be adaptive, not dogmatic. The reconciliation is found in intent. A review is not sacred; it is provisional. When it becomes mechanical, it serves the calendar instead of the work. The pulse must stay alive.

The third claim concerns blockers. Blockers are rarely dramatic; they usually take the form of small, accumulating frictions: a missing API key, a delayed procurement sign-off, a test suite that fails unpredictably. Co-operatives UK tracked blockers with a simple metric: "time to unblock". Anything that lingered more than seven days triggered an escalation. The behaviour—timestamping every blocker—turned an abstraction—risk—into something measurable.

When someone asked whether progress was at risk, the dashboard answered without emotion. A blocker older than seven days pulsed red on the screen. Clarity replaced defensiveness.

In this context, the weekly review serves as a forcing function. The 45-minute window is not long, so priorities must be crisp. Participants come prepared because the cadence expects it. Preparation becomes a habit: people update metrics before the meeting; they clarify experiments; they articulate blockers thoughtfully rather than improvising. The review is short because the work around it is disciplined.

A contrasting example from industry sharpens the point. In 2020, an Edinburgh fintech introduced a sprawling two-hour "weekly sync" with a 27-item agenda. It drained attention and obscured signal. Predictably, the meeting generated more notes than actions. Productivity analysis later showed no improvement in delivery timelines across the quarter. The limitation was not the concept of review but the loss of constraint. The pulse slowed until it barely resembled a pulse at all. This example strengthens the case for the 45-minute design: time scarcity enforces clarity.

We return to the motif. A pulse is reassuring because it repeats. That repetition allows trend-spotting. Co-operatives UK used the same dashboard for six months, adjusting only definitions, never cadence. Gradually, patterns emerged: customer-support volume spiked every third week; a specific experiment type consistently overran;

blockers doubled during onboarding cycles. These insights did not surface in any single meeting. They surfaced because the team observed the same signals, in the same format, at the same moment each week. That is the compounding effect of consistency.

As the chapter's arc progresses, the implication broadens. A weekly operating review becomes a personal discipline as much as a team practice. Individuals who adopt a similar cadence—review goals, examine experiments, track blockers—report lower stress and clearer intent. A 2022 study from the University of Leeds on knowledge-worker routines found that weekly reflection sessions correlated with a 17% increase in perceived task clarity (Leeds Work Patterns Study, 2022). Clarity is a resource. Ambiguity drains energy; rhythm restores it.

Yet there is a boundary worth articulating. Not everything belongs in the review. Some metrics distract. Some experiments need more time than a weekly update can honour. Some blockers are mere inconveniences rather than genuine risks. The discipline lies in choosing what enters the pulse. Teams that succeed draw a line: only the consequential appears on the dashboard. Everything else belongs elsewhere.

The practical consequence is profound. When a team protects the sanctity of the pulse, it builds a form of operational trust. Members know that if something matters, it will surface on Monday at 09:15. They also know that the meeting will not sprawl into unrelated commentary. This trust accumulates week by week until the review becomes an anchor point, a stabilising horizon in volatile work.

And so the unresolved question sits quietly beneath the surface. If you compressed everything that matters in your work into a single 45-minute pulse each week—one dashboard, one set of experiments, one definition of blockers—what would earn its place, and what would you finally admit no longer deserves the team's attention?

Ethical guardrails at home: Apply the same standards privately: consent, attribution, and bias checks

On a wet evening in March 2024, in a terraced house in Leeds, Sarah Whitfield sat at the kitchen table with her two teenage sons. The conversation was triggered by a message that flashed across one of their phones—an apparently candid video of a classmate arguing with a teacher. The clip looked real. It sounded real. Yet the timestamp was wrong, the lighting inconsistent, and the background warped at the edges. Within minutes, Sarah had opened a small notebook she kept for digital norms at home. She moved through three simple heuristics—"who made this?", "who gains?", "what doesn't add up?"—teaching the boys how to probe the image. By the end of the conversation, they had agreed not to share the clip and to raise it with their head of year. The next day, school staff confirmed it was a deepfake circulating among pupils. A minor crisis was avoided, and a quiet standard was set: digital life at home requires rules every bit as deliberate as those in institutions.

That evening captures a truth too often neglected: ethical guardrails are not solely matters for governments or corporations. They begin in kitchens, bedrooms, and family chats. They are formed in the micro-decisions about what we share, how we prompt, which outputs we trust, and whose consent we seek. The motif that threads through this discussion—the *threshold*—reflects the line between using technology effectively and using it carelessly. Every household crosses thresholds daily. Most do so without noticing. The aim is to notice.

The first major claim concerns consent. The Whitfield scene shows the *show*: a parent intervening before harm spreads. The *name* is household consent boundaries: a set of expectations about when and how digital tools may process another person's image, voice, or data. The *explanation* is direct. In private life, boundaries dissolve quickly because tools feel intimate; prompts feel ephemeral; and the stakes seem low. Yet the implications are concrete. In 2023, the Internet Watch Foundation reported a rise in non-consensual synthetic imagery complaints across UK schools (IWF Annual Assessment, 2023). The behaviour that prevents such misuse is simple: family members must learn to pause before generating or uploading anything involving another person. The threshold is crossed only when consent is explicit.

This leads to the second claim: attribution anchored in habit. In October 2022, University College London's Knowledge Lab observed that students who routinely labelled the origin of AI-assisted material—source file, prompt used, transformation applied—developed stronger critical reasoning than those who did not (UCL Youth Media Study, 2022). The *show* was a folder of properly attributed student work; the *name* is traceability. The *explanation* lies in how attribution forces users to recall and document decisions that otherwise vanish. The *implication*: creating a digital trail at home is not bureaucracy; it is memory. It protects against false confidence and unintended plagiarism. A household norm—"label anything assisted"—instils a discipline often missing in the workplace.

One might argue that family environments are too fluid for such norms to hold. A counter-example arises from a 2021 pilot project in Birmingham, where families were encouraged to implement lightweight digital charters. Uptake was high; adherence declined within three months. Devices multiplied; schedules slipped; the charters—two pages long—became aspirational clutter. This limitation matters. If guardrails are too elaborate, households ignore them. The reconciliation lies in scale. Guardrails must fit the grain of daily life: small, repeatable, and visible. A threshold must be easy to approach and hard to forget.

A third claim concerns bias checks. Bias sounds abstract, but its effects are visible in household decisions: which recipes surface first; which revision notes are suggested; which images tools deem "professional." In January 2023, the Ada Lovelace Institute published findings from a study on domestic AI adoption, noting that families who conducted simple counterfactual prompts—"show me the same result with a different age or accent"—were more likely to detect skewed outputs (Lovelace Domestic AI Study, 2023). The *show* is a teen comparing two generated CV templates; the *name* is counterfactual probing; the *explanation* is clear: contrasting two outputs illuminates hidden filters. The *implication*: bias checks work only when they are habitual. A threshold must be crossed with regularity, not ceremony.

The motif returns. The threshold is where attention shifts from unquestioning use to mindful engagement. At home, thresholds sit everywhere: before hitting "share"; before reusing AI-assisted text; before trusting a sensational clip. These daily pauses accumulate into a stance. Without them, private use becomes porous, subject to whichever algorithm is closest at hand.

A contrasting example highlights the stakes. In 2022, a family in Glasgow used an image-enhancing app to restore old photos for a memorial slideshow. The app subtly lightened skin tones and narrowed facial features. The family printed the images without noticing. Only later, during conversations with relatives, did they realise the distortions. No harm was intended, yet a subtle falsification entered family memory. The limitation is not technology; it is the absence of a bias threshold at the moment of choice. The reconciliation is gentle: not all distortions are malicious, but all deserve scrutiny.

Consent, attribution, and bias checks form a triad that strengthens household digital practice. But they gain force only when embedded in conversation. This is why the Whitfield kitchen scene resonates. The conversation was not a lecture; it was a joint act of interpretation. The boys were invited to inspect inconsistencies, question motives, and articulate doubts. The behaviour—dialogue rather than decree—matters. A threshold is easier to see when someone helps you approach it.

A second example deepens the point. In December 2023, a community centre in Bristol began hosting monthly "family tech circles" where parents and teens tested tools together. One session involved spotting manipulated audio. Another explored prompt structure. Participation was voluntary; attendance hovered around twenty families. Six months later, the centre noted a marked shift in how participants described their online routines: more sceptical, more articulate, and more willing to ask for verification. These are small metrics, but they chart a cultural shift: ethical guardrails become sturdier when shared.

Yet the domestic sphere also contains a tension: privacy must not be sacrificed in the name of safety. Over-monitoring erodes trust; under-monitoring invites harm. Finding the threshold between guidance and intrusion is delicate. A digital norm that works for a fifteen-year-old may be oppressive for a seventeen-year-old. A heuristic that comforts one parent may feel stifling to another. The lesson is not to enforce uniformity but to cultivate awareness. The threshold shifts; the guardrails must flex.

All this brings us to the final implication. Ethical guardrails at home are less about controlling technology and more about cultivating judgement. Tools accelerate; households must slow enough to examine their choices. Tools simplify; families must complicate their reasoning. Tools automate; people must remain accountable. And so the forward question settles quietly: when the next synthetic image, persuasive prompt, or polished output lands on your screen, which threshold will you cross—automatic use or deliberate scrutiny—and who in your household will you bring with you as you choose?

A 90-day plan: Map tasks, install guardrails, pick one leverage project, and ship

On a grey morning in May 2023, in a coworking space near Shoreditch High Street, David Patel opened a fresh notebook and wrote a date three months ahead. He had reached a point that many knowledge workers recognise but few admit: his tools were polished, his intentions sincere, yet his output lagged behind his capability. He had drafts scattered across apps, automations half-built, and an inbox that signalled busy rather than effective. A mentor suggested a simple experiment: one tightly bounded 90-day cycle with a single leverage project, measured weekly, and shipped without drama at the end. David accepted. By August, he had delivered a research brief that previously eluded him for over a year. His notebook contained three pages of lessons, each anchored in tasks mapped, guardrails installed, and one idea carried through to completion. The cycle worked.

A 90-day horizon is neither too wide to blur judgement nor too short to distort priorities. It gives shape to energy. It separates the essential from the ornamental. The motif that threads this piece—the *season*—reflects that natural rhythm. Seasons invite commitment without permanence. They carry beginnings, middles, and endings. And like seasons, 90-day plans demand pace, boundaries, and renewal.

To demonstrate the first major claim—mapping tasks brings clarity—the scene must be concrete. In June 2022, the Wellcome Collection in London invited independent researchers to pilot an "output mapping" sprint. One participant, historian Amelia Cross, documented every recurring task in her practice over a week: note capture, archival queries, citation checks, correspondence. Seeing her commitments laid out forced a choice. She reduced her active projects from nine to three and created a short index of standard prompts for complex analysis. The implication was measurable: by her own dated log, she increased the completion rate of weekly research notes from two to six. The season sharpened her judgement.

Task mapping, however, exposes a limitation. When lists become too granular, they paralyse rather than guide. This counter-example surfaced in a 2021 productivity cohort in Manchester, where several participants produced sprawling inventories of micro-tasks. Their plans stalled. The reconciliation lies not in abandoning mapping but in shaping it. A map is a decision aid, not a manuscript. It guides direction rather than accounting for every step. A season needs waypoints, not exhaustive scripts.

The second major claim—installing guardrails prevents drift—requires naming the behaviours that stabilise a cycle. In David Patel's case, guardrails took the form of a prompt journal and a version log. Every automation he built began with a short statement of purpose—one sentence, handwritten. Every revision was timestamped. These small actions prevented the familiar slide into tinkering for its own sake. The explanation is straightforward. Guardrails make choices visible. They externalise intent. The implication is cultural: a personal OS grows sturdier when decisions leave a trace.

Another example deepens this principle. In September 2023, a research team at the University of Edinburgh ran a 90-day internal trial using shared guardrails: weekly review slots, explicit consent checks for data use, and a centralised prompt library with attribution. By December, their project documentation showed fewer duplicated analyses and faster convergence in model testing. The behaviours—not the tools—created stability. The season held.

A third claim centres on the leverage project—the single effort within a cycle that shifts one's trajectory. A leverage project is not simply large. It is catalytic. David's leverage project was his research brief; Amelia's was her new archival method. The *show* is evident in their outputs. The *name* is prioritisation by impact. The *explanation* is grounded in behaviour: choosing one project means saying no to twelve. The *implication*: progress becomes lumpy rather than scattered, and the peaks matter more than the plateaus.

Yet leverage has limits. In a 2020 design cohort in Rotterdam, participants focused obsessively on one ambitious goal per cycle. Some achieved breakthroughs; others burned through their 90 days without building supporting habits. The limitation teaches a subtler reconciliation. Leverage projects must sit atop stable routines. Seasons flourish when structure meets ambition.

The fourth claim concerns shipping—finishing the cycle with a deliverable that marks the boundary between one season and the next. Shipping anchors time. It prevents the quiet decay of almost-finished work. In both the Shoreditch and Edinburgh cases, shipping was not theatrical. It was procedural. A dated export. A short retrospective. A handover or a publication. Shipping signals that the season ends and renewal begins.

This approach becomes especially vivid through the reader case requested for this subchapter. Consider "L.", a composite drawn from anonymised reader submissions between February and December 2023. L. began their first cycle by mapping tasks: researching, editing, client proposals, and four recurring admin duties. They installed three guardrails: a prompt log, a weekly metrics snapshot, and a consent checklist for any client data processed with automated tools. Their leverage project for Cycle One was building a structured reading pipeline—a simple web form feeding a database. They shipped it on Day 89, recorded the date, and wrote a brief post-mortem. Cycle Two refined this pipeline and integrated a summarisation routine. Cycle Three focused on a new capability: producing a monthly insight digest. After three seasons, L.'s measured outputs grew in consistency rather than volume: fewer abandoned drafts, smoother handoffs to clients, and clearer evidence trails. The motif holds. A season, worked through deliberately, compounds.

Throughout these examples, the rhetorical season motif underscores the same behaviour: commit for a bounded period, reflect, then reset. The cycle creates momentum without fatigue. It also builds immunity to hype. When tasks are mapped and guardrails set, new tools must prove themselves within the season. When a leverage project is chosen, novelty competes with practical value. When shipping is standard, perfectionism yields to clarity.

The final tension arrives quietly. Seasons create discipline, yet they risk rigidity if held too tightly. What happens when a breakthrough arises in week three? Should it disrupt the season or wait for the next? What if a guardrail begins to constrain rather than support? What if the leverage project loses relevance halfway through? These questions define the threshold between structure and adaptability. And so the forward test remains: as your next 90-day season approaches, which commitments deserve protection, which deserve revision, and which single project—among all the possibilities—will truly make the season worth completing?

About the Author

Kenan Durveil writes at the intersection of technology, work, and human dignity. After years helping teams adopt new tools without losing their soul, he now focuses on practical ways people can thrive alongside intelligent systems. His worldview is shaped by craft traditions and the long memory of workers who adapted to previous waves of change; the story of the Luddites is, for him, less about smashing machines and more about defending fair terms for progress. He works with small teams, educators, and public bodies to translate big ideas into everyday practice. His mission is simple: design workflows and norms where automation lifts judgement, creativity, and care rather than replacing them.

www.ingramcontent.com/pod-product-compliance
Lightning Source LLC
Chambersburg PA
CBHW031337230926
51848CB00002B/268
* 9 7 8 9 3 7 4 5 9 2 8 6 1 *